Going Public

Going Public

A Practical Guide to Public Talk

Virginia P. Richmond
West Virginia University

Mark Hickson III
University of Alabama at Birmingham

Allyn and Bacon

Boston ■ London ■ Toronto ■ Sydney ■ Tokyo ■ Singapore

Senior Editor: Karon Bowers
Editorial Assistant: Jennifer Trebby
Marketing Manager: Mandee Eckersley
Editorial-Production Service: Omegatype Typography, Inc.
Composition and Prepress Buyer: Linda Cox
Manufacturing Buyer: Julie McNeill
Cover Administrator: Kristina Mose-Libon
Electronic Composition: Omegatype Typography, Inc.

Library of Congress Cataloging-in-Publication Data

Richmond, Virginia P.
    Going public : a practical guide to public talk / Virginia P. Richmond, Mark Hickson
III.—1st ed.
      p. cm.
    Includes bibliographical references and index.
    ISBN 0-205-32263-8 (alk. paper)
    1. Public speaking.   I. Hickson, Mark.   II. Title.
PN4129.15 .R53 2002
808.5'1—dc21

                                                      2001045092

Printed in the United States of America

10 9 8 7 6 5 4 3 2 1   06 05 04 03 02 01

*This book is dedicated to
James C. McCroskey,
West Virginia University,
whose ideas inspired its writing.*

CONTENTS

PREFACE

The art of public speaking has been around for more than 2,500 years. During the intervening time, a variety of textbooks have addressed how such an art can be improved, although some talent is needed in the beginning. Little has been written, however, about the science of public speaking. Although this textbook does not address the scientific elements of improving the voice, for example, it does address public speaking as an activity that can be approached with scientific discipline. From the beginning, this book focuses upon how one can become a better talker—a good speaker—when the principles outlined are implemented. This text is not for the excellent speaker to become superior, nor is it a history of the teaching of public speaking. Instead, it is a practical, everyday resource manual that assists those with little experience in becoming proficient.

A number of self-help tests are provided in this text that allow the potential speaker to analyze strengths and weaknesses and determine information about the audience—all of which increase one's confidence.

The chapters are in an order that allows the neophyte an opportunity to begin practice early in the process. Chapter 1 provides a background, while Chapter 2 is an overview of the speech making process in synopsis form. Chapters 3 and 4 delineate methods for analyzing and overcoming one's fears. Chapters 5 and 6 illustrate methods for analyzing the speaker and the audience. Chapter 7 recognizes the importance of listening in the public speaking situation. Chapter 8 focuses on elements of delivery, including gestures and vocalics. Chapter 9 provides insight into the kinds of language that should and should not be used in a public speaking context. Chapter 10 discusses the research materials available to prepare a speech, including library sources and electronic media sources. Chapter 11 explains how the research materials discovered in Chapter 10 should be used in the speech. Chapter 12 is a synopsis of the various types of audio and visual aids that can be used in support of the speech. Chapter 13 provides an innovative method for organizing the materials used in a speech. Chapter 14 outlines the similarities and differences in four different types of speeches that are used in everyday life. The book ends with two appendixes: Appendix A is a discussion of the ethics of what should and should not be done when talking at the public level, and Appendix B is a series of evaluation forms used for a variety of different types of speeches.

In each chapter, we have focused on providing a practical method for developing, organizing, preparing, and delivering a speech. We hope that *Going Public: A Practical Guide to Public Talk* will be a valuable tool for the student as a student, and for the student who becomes a professional.

Acknowledgments

We would like to thank Pam Short, University of Alabama at Birmingham, for her photographs and artwork. We would like to thank Carol T. Adams, University of Alabama at Birmingham, for her help in proofreading the manuscript. We would also like to express our appreciation to Leighanne Heisel, University of Missouri at St. Louis, Alan D. Heisel, University of Missouri at St. Louis, and Kristin M. Valencic, West Virginia University for writing the instructor's manual for this textbook. We would also like to thank the reviewers of this edition for their insightful comments and suggestions: Jerry Allen, University of New Haven; Charles J. G. Griffin, Kansas State University; Joel Patterson, DeVry Institute of Technology; Nan Peck, Northern Virginia Community College; Marc Skinner, University of Idaho; and Archie Wortham, St. Philip's College.

Going Public

1

Why Public Talk?

"Carlos, it's your turn to speak." These may be among the most dreaded words a college student ever hears. What Carlos must do—and what all students of public speaking must do—is to air his views and knowledge in a public situation. No doubt, Carlos offers his opinions about the upcoming and the previous hoop games. He tells his friends what movies he likes and dislikes. Carlos may even share his views on political crises and legal matters, despite his limited knowledge of these topics.

What makes this situation different is that it takes place in a *public* forum. That is, many people listen to what Carlos has to say. He has the floor. What he says and how he says it tell the others in the audience something about Carlos's speech topic. More importantly, his talk tells them something about Carlos.

Most students feel that public speaking class is to be dreaded because it is frightening or because they believe it is not important for the rest of their lives. However, following school, almost everyone has occasion to speak in public. Public speaking is important for political reasons, economic reasons, instructional reasons, and professional reasons. The purpose of this text is to illustrate how public speaking is important to the college student and the college graduate. In the process of discussing its importance, we illustrate a few ways to make public speaking more effective in the contexts in which you will use it.

Political Reasons for Public Speaking

Once you graduate you will most likely obtain a job or another job and you may move to a different location. Where you live will be important. For the protection of your home and your investment in that home, you may have to speak to a zoning commission to prevent a shopping center's building, a strip joint, or some other objectionable entity such as a polluting industry from entering your residential area. You may want to speak out against increased sales taxes or in favor of a school board bond referendum.

Should you become involved in politics, you would deliver numerous speeches to local civic groups. As a good citizen, you might speak out about increases in costs of cable television, water prices, electrical rates, and the like. Simply being a political consumer means that you have a responsibility to know how to present your views in public.

Economic Reasons for Public Speaking

Certainly taxes and electrical rates are economic reasons as well as political reasons. But you have even greater economic reasons for learning how to speak in public. You may have to speak to a union meeting about wages and benefits. As a professional, you may be required to attend meetings with others in your workplace to discuss hours, benefits, or company closings. Virtually every dollar that you earn and spend may become a public issue, and you should be prepared to enter the forum at any time.

Instructional Reasons for Public Speaking

If there is a subject about which you are an expert, other issues arise for which you may speak. It may be about a hobby such as fly fishing, CD collecting, baseball memorabilia, or coin collecting. In the workplace you may have to explain to your colleagues how to weld or how to build a deck. As a professional, you may have to explain to other lawyers the minute details of a case involving a client. As a physician, you may have to explain how to perform triple bypass heart surgery. At church, you may deliver a lay sermon or be asked to teach a Sunday School class. Everyone needs to know and understand the process of presenting information and persuading in public.

In this chapter, we discuss what makes public talk what it is—how it is different from a conversation or an argument among friends. We briefly discuss the major elements of a speech (calling it "public talk"), and we outline the remainder of the book. We begin by discussing seven fallacies of public talk, some of which make public speaking seem so difficult.

Professional Reasons for Public Speaking

Many people make a substantial portion of their living by delivering public talks. Clergy, attorneys, and teachers immediately come to mind. Human relations personnel often speak to employees about benefits and company policy. Public relations people find speaking an important part of their jobs. Many of the people in these positions never thought they would be professional communicators when they took public speaking in college. Most, though, attribute much of their career success to this course and what they learned from it.

Many students believe that there are natural abilities associated with being an effective public speaker. Certainly there are factors that make one speaker sound better than another, but the art of public speaking requires more than natural talent. In addition, those with natural talent are not necessarily the most effective. A good speaker must have some talent, along with experience and education in the art. It is the responsibility of this class to provide an opportunity for two of these three. The natural ability fallacy is but one of the myths about public speaking. We have decided to discuss seven of them.

In addition to these reasons, you may give a speech for personal reasons. You may have to give a brief speech to some group when you are giving or receiving an award. You may have to give a speech as part of a roast of a friend's retirement or fiftieth birthday party. You may offer a toast at a wedding reception. Thus, there are also personal reasons for learning to deliver an effective speech.

Seven Fallacies of Public Talk

Speakers Are Born, Not Made.   When the art of public talk began more than two thousand years ago, the notion was that public talk was to be used by Greek men who held high places as lawyers and politicians. The early Greeks needed first to create and maintain democracy in new nation-states, such as Athens. The theorists of the times felt that good speaking was composed of a natural ability, learning the art, and the hard work of practice and experience. We must remember, however, that the first of these—natural ability—was important primarily because speakers had to speak loudly to be heard. In today's world of microphones, though, even Broadway actors find it unnecessary to practice the fine art of projecting through a loud voice.

Since those early times in Greece, the teaching of public talk has become an asset available to virtually everyone. By studying the good speakers of the past, we now have the tools to teach and learn how to overcome most natural limitations of a speaker. The Greeks' other two requirements of the orator, however, remain. A good speaker must learn the art and must practice.

Most People Feel Comfortable Talking in Public.   As we learn in another chapter, this is definitely not the case. Most people who talk in public find it something for which they must prepare. Although public speaking is the number-one fear of most Americans, this is because most people do not really understand the basics of the art of public talk. In addition, many people feel comfortable presenting information to some groups but not others. For example, an attorney might feel uncomfortable teaching a religious class.

A Speaker Must Memorize the Speech or Read It Word for Word.   A speaker does not have to and should not memorize a speech. That is what actors do. Neither should a speaker write out a speech and read it word for word. The art of reading in public is a separate art from that of talking in public, and the two should not be confused with each other. You will note in this book that we rarely advocate that a speaker should write the speech word for word.

One Should Always Begin a Speech with a Joke.   This has been a traditional method for loosening up both the speaker and the audience, but quite frankly, it rarely works. Many speakers are not naturally humorous. Sarcasm and satire are often misunderstood in a speech and therefore make it worse than it might have been otherwise. In addition, many of the jokes that are told are out-of-date, too gross, sexist, or racist, and end up hurting the feelings of those in the audience more often than they generate humor.

The Content of the Speech Is a Secondary Aspect of the Speech.   Many students believe that another student who looks as though he or she feels comfortable and who speaks with a good voice and has appropriate gestures will make the best grades in the class. Nothing could be further from the truth. The most important element for a speech is the content of the talk. In a few days the audience members forget what you wore, how good your voice was, or how comfortable you appeared. They will remember much of the speech itself, if the talk has been well prepared and the audience members felt it was about something they needed to know.

Public Speaking Is a Formal Process in Which the Speaker Should Always Stand, in One Place, Behind a Lectern.   The time may come when you will deliver a speech in a tuxedo or a formal dress, but this is not a requirement of public speaking in general. There are times when standing in one place might be effective, but most often it is not. What a speaker wears and where he or she stands have less to do with overall effectiveness than does the content of the speech.

A Person Can Learn How to Deliver an Effective Speech by Reading a Book on the Topic.   Certainly we hope that this book will assist you in preparing an effective public talk, but the guidance of an able instructor and substantial practice are needed to create the most effective public talk.

What Is Public Talk?

The first, and most obvious, aspect of public talk is the number of people who are listening to one speaker for a set amount of time. Second, this form of communication is related to the length of time that one person has the floor. Third, public speaking differs from conversation in the type of language that is used. Fourth, the audience has different expectations when they are listening together than were they to listen individually. Fifth, public talk requires substantial preparation before the speaker begins.

The Nature of the Public

There are several different types of communication based on the number of people you are communicating with, the context, and the amount of time utilized by one individual. *Intrapersonal communication* involves those times when you are talking to yourself, usually prior to talking with someone else: What is the right thing to say? Which word should I use? This conversation goes on within your mind, and words are never uttered. *Interpersonal communication* involves talking to another person in an informal context, with *informal* meaning that the message is taken less seriously—it is not on the record. Telephone conversations and interviews are examples of interpersonal communication.

    Small group communication usually involves three to twelve people. Juries, committee meetings, and work units are examples in which small group communication takes place. The people are usually together for a specific purpose and the context begins becoming more formal. Often records are kept of such interactions. *Public speaking* most often involves more than twelve people; the context is more formal. There are often records kept of these events. Thus, as communication becomes more public, the context becomes more formal and the number of persons involved increases. Additionally, the percentage of time spent speaking by one individual increases.

Holding the Public Floor

When an individual delivers a speech in public, the attendees expect that speaker to do most of the talking. In many cases, the audience members have paid a fee to hear what this person has to say. Usually they are not interested in what the others in the audience have to say, unless there are questions that elucidate what the speaker has already said. The speaker is the focus of attention of the audience. Because each audience member is investing his or her time (and perhaps money), each has certain expectations of the speaker. Just as many students become upset when two or three students monopolize a class, audiences do the same.

Language in Public

In everyday conversation, we often engage in street talk or mall talk. This talk includes some words that might be offensive to others. It includes trite expressions such as "you know" and "like." It includes the language of subculture and varies considerably from time to time. A *home* might become a *pad. Money* might become *coins. Bad* might mean *good.* Nevertheless, the language that we use in public is much more conservative. A speaker's language should be traditional, precise, concise, specific, clear, and interesting. He or she should not use "in" words, profanities, obscenities, or abstractions. The main reason for this is that public audiences are more diverse and the likelihood of offending someone is increased. In addition, because public speaking is more formal, its language must take on some different characteristics. At the same time, though, the words should sound as if they are part of the speaker's natural, "normal" vocabulary.

Audience Expectations

If you were to go to a basketball practice session at your college, you might have certain expectations. For example, you would not expect the players to be wearing their game uniforms. You would not expect the band and cheerleaders to be there. You would not expect the game to go for two, twenty-minute halves. You would have these expectations because you know this is not a "real" game. The coach would stop the players frequently to point out mistakes. If, though, you attended a game with twelve thousand others watching, you would expect all of the "bells and whistles." The cheerleaders and band would be there. All of the participants would be dressed in the team's colors. The time clock would be used precisely.

Such is the difference between conversation and going public. In a conversation we do not usually expect a certain amount of time to be used. We do not expect that the other person will provide evidence and argument for her opinions. But in a public speech we anticipate the *best* from the person who holds the floor. Part of this is a group phenomenon. The group as a whole expects the speaker to do his or her best. Other group members are expected to be quiet and polite while this person is talking. The speaker is expected to notify us of where information came from, especially if it is controversial.

Speaker Preparation

For all of the reasons given, the speaker is expected to be at his or her best. Thus, much like the basketball team, the speaker must prepare for his or her speech. Such preparation means ensuring that the speech will be within the time limits imposed, not too long, not too short. The speaker is expected to have all of his visual aids in working order. He or she must provide information that is not well known to the audience. In short, the speaker is expected to make the speech a learning experience for those who are listening to him.

Even in those cases in which one's public talk may be brief (what is referred to as an impromptu speech), a significant amount of preparation is necessary. For example, if a citizen is arguing not to have a retail store in his neighborhood, his argument for not changing the property restrictions must have some legal basis. In addition, he should carefully choose his words and should talk for an appropriate amount of time. His gestures and facial expressions must be consistent with the message that he is creating. The speaker should also be concerned about his credibility, illustrating that he is trustworthy and competent. Finally, he needs to demonstrate that his goodwill is for the community, not just for himself. These factors may take years of preparation in having confidence in what one is saying, ensuring rapport with the audience, and having memory of previous experiences with similar types of situations.

SUMMARY

Public speaking is important for your daily lives. It affects your political situation as well as your economic situation. Public speaking is integral to instruction and for the professions. Yet most people believe several fallacies about what public speaking is and what it does. You now know, though, that effective public speakers become so because of training and experience. Although most people will engage in public speaking, many do not feel especially comfortable in doing so. Public speaking is not like acting, and you should not try to write out or memorize most speeches. Although it may be helpful, natural talent such as having a good voice it not essential for effectively speaking in public. The content is the most important part of a speech.

From this chapter, it has become obvious that public speaking is different from other types of talk. One person talks longer to more people. He or she uses a different style of language. The public speaker prepares for a public talk more so than for a private talk. All of these factors make for a successful experience. The remaining chapters discuss each of these elements and others in more detail.

CHAPTER

2

The Basics

11

Public speaking is the least common of the four primary forms of oral communication: public speaking, participating as a member of a large group or class, interacting in small groups, conversing in dyads. In the past, few people gave more than a handful of formal public speeches in their entire lives. Currently, anyone might be asked to "go public" anywhere at any time. National surveys of U.S. citizens have found public speaking to be their number-one fear.

Many students have already given a few speeches by the time they enter college, but they may think they have given far fewer than they have. Speech making is a common activity in elementary and secondary schools, although it often goes under other names: show and tell, oral reading, oral book reports, current events, and science projects.

Some schools offer formal classes in public speaking, and many have debate and forensics programs for students who want to polish their speaking skills. However, most students have had no formal training in public speaking. They have been expected to speak in public with no training and often have been publicly evaluated on their performance. It is not surprising, then, that people feel apprehensive about having to do something they do not know how to do in front of others.

This chapter is not designed to ensure that you will be a polished public speaker. It is designed to give you a more realistic perspective on your chances of being a successful speaker. This chapter points to the basic skills that you can master to speak in public with some confidence and success.

The Nature of Public Speaking

Public speaking is oral communication in a one-to-many, one-way format that suggests only one person is acting as the main source of verbal and nonverbal messages at a given time, but many are receivers. Although, theoretically at least, a public speech could be given with only one person, or a small group, being present, in actual practice such would not be likely to happen. The speaker and the audience member (or small group) would probably switch into dyadic (or small group) interaction under such circumstances. The planned public speech would most likely not be given as planned.

The number of people in the audience for a public speech may vary from a few to a few hundred, if the speaker can speak loudly or when a microphone is available. It may even grow to a few thousand. It may grow to several million with the assistance of radio, television, and/or film. This chapter restricts content to the live, nonmediated level of public speaking, which is the situation most of us will encounter.

When we use the term *monological*, we are referring to the public speaker being the only person talking for a given period—the length of the speech. This is the normal pattern for public speaking, although many experienced speakers, especially when talking to small audiences, will invite audience members to stop them to ask questions or add comments. However, audiences usually do not expect such an invitation to interrupt, and without that invitation most people will avoid breaking in because it is considered very rude. It is much more common for people to hold any questions or comments until the speaker has finished and formally requests such interaction with the audience.

Often there is more than one speaker present. Such formats as symposiums, panel presentations, or debates provide for serial monologues—one person speaking after another. These are generally quite formal occasions in which no one is expected to interrupt. The audience often is invited to ask questions after all the speakers have completed their presentations.

Although not included in our definition of public speaking, feedback typically is an important factor in nonmediated public speaking events. *Feedback* permits the speaker to judge how his or her ideas are being received and allows adaptation during the speech to make it more effective; feedback involves the verbal and nonverbal responses the audience provides to the speaker. How the audience responds not only has a major impact on the speaker (Gardiner, 1972) but also can have a strong influence on the members of the audience (Hylton, 1971).

These three characteristics of public speaking (monological, large number of receivers, and availability of feedback) provide important advantages to the communicator. Because public speaking is monological, the speaker can carefully prepare in advance so the verbal message will say exactly what he or she wants it to say. Having many receivers permits greater impact with less effort than would be necessary to contact each audience member individually or in small groups. Having available feedback permits the speaker to adjust the verbal and nonverbal messages to fit the audience and increase the chances of achieving the purpose of the speech.

There are two disadvantages of the public speaking format. The first is that it usually is noninteractive. Therefore, the feedback obtained is all nonverbal. Misunderstandings and disagreements by audience members may not become known to the speaker. Therefore, the speech may fail without the speaker knowing that it has, much less why it has failed. This disadvantage can be overcome, however, if the speaker can draw the audience into the transaction by asking questions and making comments. In this way, the interactive nature of interpersonal communication replaces the monological nature of public speaking.

The second disadvantage is that this communication context is likely to be accompanied by much higher apprehension by the speaker than any other context. This problem can be dealt with if the speaker can gain an accurate perspective on the public speaking process.

Gaining Perspective

Fear of the unknown is normal. Remember when you were a child and became frightened when the lights were turned off? What happened when the lights were turned back on? If you were like most children (or adults for that matter), the fear went away immediately when you saw there was nothing to fear.

Fear or anxiety about public speaking is much like fear of the dark. If you do not know "what is out there waiting for you," it is reasonable to be fearful and anxious. For most, however, when the light is turned on, the "scary thing" goes away. Reading this chapter can help you gain perspective and therefore gain more control. The more you know about the public speaking process, the more light is shed on what was previously the unknown. Many books explain the public communication process in considerable detail (e.g., McCroskey, 1997). Reading such a book can add a great deal of light to the situation, as can taking a formal course in public speaking.

There are two things you should remember. First, many people are asked to give speeches in their lives, and when they are, it often is not possible to refuse with no major penalty. Second, if you are one of those who must give speeches, you can learn more about the process and as you gain more experience, you will likely get better at it—and become less fearful.

Look up your scores on the PRCA (Table 3.3, on page 35). Check to see what your score is on the public speaking dimension. A score above 18 indicates you feel a good bit of apprehension about speaking in this context. Be aware that if you score between 18 and 30 you are normal. That is where most people of all ages score.

Yes, most people are apprehensive about giving speeches. When you watch and listen to them speak you may or may not be aware they are frightened. If you recognize their fear, how do you feel about them? If you answer, "Sympathetic," you are like most people. That is how most people will also feel about you if you appear frightened while speaking before them. Just like you would be if you were in the audience, they are cheering for you and hoping you will succeed.

Finally, you need to recognize there is no such thing as fear, anxiety, stage fright, or whatever you want to call it. These are only labels people use to represent their physiological activation. Others use labels such as *excitement, thrill,* and *exhilaration* to represent the same feelings. The difference is in one's mind. If you can change the label, you probably can change the experience. Fear of public speaking, or the thrill of public speaking, is analogous to the fear of roller coasters, or the thrill of roller coasters. People who fear such rides and those who are thrilled by such rides experience much the same physiological reaction. They simply give it different labels and experience it differently. Recognize that as you approach a public speaking opportunity, your body is becoming physiologically aroused to allow you to be "on top of your game" as you talk to your audience. Recognizing that activation as your friend, rather than your enemy, will go a long way toward making stage fright a memory rather than a presence.

The Basic Skills

To become an outstanding and highly effective public speaker is not easy, but it can be done with motivation, study, skills, experience, and fear reduction. You probably need to set excellence in public speaking as one of your goals. For example, if you plan to be a corporate recruiter, personnel manager, public relations expert, advertising executive, marketing expert, corporate trainer, foundation manager, development officer, member of the clergy, trial attorney, candidate for political office, lawyer, or college professor, or if you enter another occupation that requires you to be a professional public speaker, you should seek instruction in public speaking. Try to get as much experience in as many different public speaking settings as you can while you are in school. Such training and experience are quite costly outside the college environment.

If your needs in the public speaking context are less formidable, you probably can become a satisfactory speaker for most occasions by learning a few basics. Mastery of these basics can make public speaking one of your basic skills and prepare you to deal with most public speaking demands in everyday life. These basics include topic selection, speech organization, and delivery. We consider each in turn.

Topic Selection

Choosing a topic for a speech is often intimidating to people taking classes in public speaking. They just do not know what to talk about. Their plight is real. They are not motivated to talk at all, about anything. They have no purpose to accomplish. They may feel that the class does not really want to hear them talk about anything either. Worse yet, they may feel they really do not know anything the other class members do not also know. They cannot choose the option that any sensible person would choose in the real world—refuse the invitation to speak!

The choice of topic for a speech usually is an easy task in everyday life. You seek the opportunity to speak because you have a purpose to accomplish that is important to you. Others request that you speak to them because they believe that you have expertise or views that they will benefit from by hearing you. In either case, you will know what you are talking about, or the public speaking opportunity is highly unlikely to arise. If you do not have an objective to accomplish, or if some other people do not believe you have something important to share with them—no speech.

It is important to keep in mind that motivation determines the value of public speaking. If you want to motivate a group of people to do something, it is a good idea to make a speech to them concerning what you want. If a group wants you to speak to them, and some benefit to you is promised or implicit, making the speech might be a good idea. If you want to do someone a favor, such altruism may justify your making the speech. Otherwise, face it, why not refuse (or not seek) the invitation? In the real world, then, the choice of topic is usually a given. It is something you know about and something you have reason to be motivated to talk about.

Speech Organization

Speeches have three parts: introduction, body, and conclusion.

The Body of the Speech.   The body of the speech should be prepared first; then it will be relatively easy to introduce it and conclude it. The body contains the main content. Generally, speeches can be organized in one of two ways (although other options are discussed later): topical sequence or motivated sequence. The first type is best for speeches in which you are trying to explain something: to give information, to brief the listeners. The second type is best when you are trying to get the audience to accept a new idea or way of doing things: to influence or persuade the audience.

Topical Sequence.   The topical sequence involves dividing the content into its logical subpoints. Each subpoint is a major idea for your speech. There should never be more than a few such subpoints—three to five in most speeches. They may be organized in arbitrary categories (oranges, watermelons, and grapes) or by some system that arises out of the topic. Examples include past, present, and future; African issues, European issues, Asian and Australian issues, South American issues, and North American issues; female behaviors, male behaviors, and gay and lesbian behaviors; before 1800, the nineteenth century, and the twentieth century; hereditary diseases, viral diseases, and bacterial diseases.

   Topical sequences emerge from an examination of the topic itself. Usually the order that should be used is clear. If it is not, that probably means the order will make little difference, as long as you make sure the audience can move from subtopic to subtopic along with you.

Motivated Sequence.   The motivated sequence that Monroe introduced into the study of communication about sixty years ago remains one of the most useful organizational patterns yet devised (Gronbeck, McKerrow, Ehninger, & Monroe, 1994). It is particularly well suited to the speech designed to elicit change in behavior. It includes five steps: attention, need, satisfaction, visualization, and action.

1. *Attention step.*   This essentially is the introduction to the speech. It is designed to get the audience in the mood to hear what the speaker has to say.
2. *Need step.*   This is the first step in the body of the speech. It addresses what is wrong with what is currently going on, what the problem is. It identifies causes and effects, and explains them to the audience.

3. *Satisfaction step.*   This is the solution to the problem that is outlined in the need step. The solution itself is explained and then it is related to the problem so that the audience can see how it would satisfy the need for a change. Enough detail should be provided to be certain the audience understands how the solution will work, but not so much as to overwhelm them with details.

4. *Visualization step.*   This step functions as a transition from the body of the speech to the conclusion. It helps the audience see what things should be like once this solution has been put in place. Positive visualization outlines the good consequences of the proposed solution being adopted. Negative visualization, in contrast, outlines the bad consequences of the proposed solution not being adopted.

5. *Action step.*   This step lets the audience know exactly what is expected of them, when, and how. It includes an appeal to them to behave in certain ways. This step is normally called the conclusion to the speech.

The topical and motivated sequences should be adequate for most speeches you will deliver. They are simple and straightforward. They help make your speech clear and avoid audience confusion.

When developing the body of the speech, always remember the KISS injunction—keep it simple, speaker! As one cynic once put it, "No one ever failed at public speaking by underestimating the ability of their audience to understand." Listening to a speech is not like reading a technical manual. If you do not get it right the first time, there is no going back over it. Therefore, clarity and simplicity are very positive virtues in a public speech.

Introducing the Speech.   The purpose of the introduction to the speech is to capture audience attention and direct that attention toward the following content. Generally, that means you should tell your audience what you are going to talk about and why. Emphasis should be placed on why they should care about what you are going to say. If they cannot see why they should care, they most likely will not listen to you. The first few sentences are like the first few seconds as one passes by television channels using a remote control.

The two primary reasons introductions fail is that the speaker thinks it is necessary either to apologize for not being a good speaker ("unaccustomed as I am to public speaking. . . .") or to tell a "funny" joke ("on the way over here today I encountered two Democrats and two Republicans . . .").

Be assured, if you are a lousy speaker, you will not need to inform the audience of that. They will figure it out soon enough. Your apology will not overcome the fact that you have wasted their time or bored them to tears. On the other hand, without the warning, they may not notice your shortcomings at all, particularly if you really are an adequate speaker.

Fill out the Richmond Communication Humor Scale in Table 2.1 and score it according to the instructions. Most people score between 50 and 65 on this scale. Our advice is that if you do not score at least 70 on this scale, you should never try to introduce a speech with a joke. Few things are more deadly as an introduction than a joke that bombs. Few rookie public speakers can tell a joke while introducing a speech. If you are not one of those unusual people, leave the jokes to the comedians.

The humor scale is the first of several scales in this textbook. These scales are mostly for you to be able to analyze your own abilities. In this case, you are analyzing your humor for public consumption. You may be very funny at times with friends, but remember public speaking usually involves an audience of very different people.

Concluding the Speech.   When approaching the conclusion of a speech, it is good to keep in mind the three Ss of public speaking: Stand up, Speak up, and Shut up. These three injunctions roughly relate to the introduction, body, and conclusion of the speech, respectively. Many speakers find the final injunction to be the most difficult to follow—they just cannot sit down and shut up. You hear them say, "in conclusion," but ten minutes later they are still rambling.

Usually when speakers have a hard time concluding it is because they have not planned their conclusion in advance. They may have worked on the body of the speech, and even the introduction, but thought the conclusion would just take care of itself. It will not.

The primary function of the conclusion is to let the audience know what you most want them to remember or do. The conclusion should be focused on that objective. Sometimes it is good to summarize the main points you have discussed. In other cases, the conclusion should focus on exactly what you want the audience to do or think.

Just as you should not apologize in your introduction, do not thank your audience in your conclusion—unless you really have imposed on them. If you sought them out and encouraged them to come to hear you,

TABLE 2.1   Richmond Communication Humor Scale (RCHS)

Directions: The following statements apply to how various people communicate humor when relating to others. Indicate in the space at the left of each item the degree to which the statement applies to you.

> 5 = Strongly Agree
> 4 = Agree
> 3 = Undecided
> 2 = Disagree
> 1 = Strongly Disagree

_____ 1. I regularly communicate with others in a group by telling jokes or amusing stories.

_____ 2. People usually laugh when I tell a joke or humorous story.

_____ 3. I cannot remember funny stories, jokes, or amusing quips.

_____ 4. I can be amusing or humorous without having to go over a joke.

_____ 5. Being funny is a natural communication orientation for me.

_____ 6. I cannot relate an amusing story well.

_____ 7. People seldom ask me to tell jokes, amusing stories, or humorous ideas.

_____ 8. My friends would say that I am a humorous or funny person.

_____ 9. People do not seem to pay close attention when I relate a joke or funny story.

_____ 10. Even funny jokes and stories seem dull when I tell them.

_____ 11. I can easily remember jokes and humorous stories.

_____ 12. People often ask me to tell jokes and amusing stories.

_____ 13. My friends would say I am not a funny person.

_____ 14. I do not tell funny stories, even when asked to do so.

_____ 15. I relate amusing stories, jokes, and funny things very well to others.

_____ 16. Of all the people I know, I am one of the "least" amusing.

_____ 17. I use humor to communicate in a variety of situations.

_____ 18. On a regular basis, I do not communicate with others by telling jokes or humorous stories.

Scoring

Step 1: Add the scores for items 3, 6, 7, 9, 10, 13, 14, 16, and 18.
Step 2: Add the scores for items 1, 2, 4, 5, 8, 11, 12, 15, and 17.
Step 3: RCHS = 48 + score from Step 2 − score from Step 1.

TABLE 2.1   Continued

Scores may range from 18 to 90.

If your score does not fall between these extremes, you have made a scoring error.

Scores above 70 indicate a high communication humor orientation.

Scores below 40 indicate a low communication humor orientation.

such as happens for a political candidate, a gracious thank you is certainly in order. However, often people say thanks because they cannot think of anything else to say at the end. Plan. It may be harder to shut up than you think.

Delivering the Speech

Preparing the speech is one thing; delivering it is quite another. For the most part, anyone with a modicum of intelligence can prepare a good speech. As you have seen by reading the previous sections, readying a speech is not that hard. But actually standing up there and giving it—that is where many people fail.

As you probably have guessed by now, delivering a speech really is not too difficult either. Let us begin with the advice that is easiest to follow.

1. *Never write out and read (or try to memorize) your speech.*   This is the rule unless your speech will occur in a very formal situation in which any misstatement could have very serious repercussions. Presidents and other officials do write some speeches because they have foreign relations ramifications. Actors memorize their speeches so that their talk seems more realistic. When we respond to someone else's speech or when we are asked a question, we may give an impromptu response, which means that we know what we want to say because we have thought about it a long time. The exact words, however, are chosen on the spur of the moment. Generally, though, public speakers use extemporaneous speaking, which means that they have an outline and know what they wish to say, but they neither read nor memorize the exact words.

2. *Have notes showing your main ideas so that if you have a mental block you can quickly get yourself on track.*   Some novice speakers are so intent on being fully prepared they write out their entire speech so nothing will be forgotten. This practice virtually ensures a poor presentation. Few of us are trained to be good oral readers. Therefore, the reading will sound awkward and cause the audience to question your competence. People often make this mistake at professional conventions. As a result, many sessions are poorly attended, many people leave during presentations, and often the few people in the audience are totally bored.

Even if a speaker is a good reader, one of the big advantages of the public speaking context—feedback—is lost. While reading, it is hard to also keep in touch with audience feedback. And even if feedback is noticed, there is little the reading speaker can do about it. Adaptation is really not possible—the speech is already there, to be read word for word.

The only thing worse than reading is memorizing the speech. If you have the slightest tendency to be nervous, forget ever memorizing your speech. Nothing makes memory go away faster than a little nervousness. Standing in front of an audience not remembering what to say next has to be one of the most unpleasant experiences a person could have.

Instead of reading or memorizing, we recommend you present your speech extemporaneously. Do not confuse this with impromptu speaking. When your speech is impromptu, you have *no* advance preparation. You are called on; you speak. You must prepare as you go along. Extemporaneous speaking, in contrast, includes *careful prep* (preparation), following the advice in the previous sections. The speaker will have the main points of the speech outlined on note cards, which he or she holds or places conveniently nearby on a table, desk, or lectern. Do not attempt to hide the notes. The audience will know you have notes—and they could not care less, unless you appear to be sneaking peaks at them. Have them and use them.

Having notes and speaking extemporaneously permit you to do the most important thing to ensure effective delivery: to be immediate with your audience. Immediacy is at the core of effective communication. Get close to your audience. Avoid standing behind a lectern, do not use a microphone unless absolutely necessary, and avoid electrical audiovisual aids whenever you can. If you must show something to the audience, give them a handout. That way they can continue to pay attention to you while you explain what is on the handout (as opposed to frantically trying to write down notes from your visual aid). Murphy's law is virtually absolute for novice speakers: If the electronic device upon which you depend can break down, it will break down. All electronic devices can break down. You must be prepared for that eventuality if you use visual aids. If you think you must impress your audience with your sharp slides or overheads or video graphics, consider impressing them with your attractive hand-outs. The effect will be much more lasting, because the handouts go home with the audience members.

Immediate delivery includes maintaining eye contact with your audience when you are not glancing at your notes. Never let audience members feel they can look away from you without your noticing their inattention. By demanding their eye contact you ensure their attention. If you do not look at them, they will stop looking at you and eventually stop paying attention to you. Do not give them that chance.

Extemporaneous, immediate delivery permits you to interact with your audience rather than just present your speech. If the audience is not too large, you can invite them to ask questions while you are talking with (not at) them. This gives the public speaking event the atmosphere and electricity of the interpersonal interaction and permits you to adapt to the responses of the audience. Remember, if you forget where you are, you have your notes nearby.

It is also important to remember other aspects of immediacy:

- Move around the room rather than stand still in one place—but avoid pacing back and forth.
- Face the audience directly as much as possible.
- Use meaningful gestures, but avoid gestures that will distract the audience (hand to face gestures, covering your face, clicking a pen).
- Wear apparel that is appropriate but not too formal.
- Avoid wearing artifacts that may distract the audience.
- Watch your use of time; going substantially overtime is very discourteous and is virtually certain to cause a loss of attention.
- Use lots of vocal variety; nothing kills attention like a monotonous voice.

If these suggestions sound a lot like advice one would give to a person who asks how to be a good conversationalist, that is no accident. These are the same communication skills, only applied to slightly different communication contexts. Effective delivery in public speaking is immediate, interpersonal delivery.

Handling Questions

The final aspect of many public speaking events is responding to questions from the audience members. Of course, questions need not be held until the end unless you have some good reason to do so. The way to handle questions is the same in either case. We recommend the following.

1. *Repeat the question before answering it.* This accomplishes two things. First, people sitting behind the questioner are not likely to hear the question otherwise. Second, in case you have misunderstood the question, the questioner has the opportunity to clear up the confusion before you waste time answering the wrong question.
2. *Be direct with your answer, if possible.* Do not attempt to evade answering a question. If you do not want to answer it, say so and explain why. Otherwise, just answer the question.
3. *Do not be afraid to say you do not know.* Never try to bluff. If you do not know, say so. Audiences usually are very understanding when a speaker acknowledges that he or she does not have all the answers. Sometimes it is effective to tell the questioner you do not know but will try to find out and get back to him or her with an answer later. Of course, it is acceptable to speculate about what the answer might be—if you clearly indicate that is what you are doing.
4. *Try to take questions from various parts of the audience.* People of like mind often sit together in an audience. To get as much variety in perspectives as possible, move around the room when picking questioners.
5. *If possible, stay after the scheduled concluding time so that other audience members may ask questions.* Sometimes speakers run out of time before some important questions get asked. In other cases, some people who really want to ask just cannot bring themselves to do so in front of all of the other people, but they can ask questions one-on-one. Give them that opportunity if you can.

Recognize that the more immediate you are, the more effective you are likely to be. Also, the more effective you are, the more likely people will have questions. If no one has a question for you, it may be because you have been so clear there just is nothing more to ask. Or it may be because the audience members are so bored they just want to get it over and get out of there. Usually it is easy to tell which is the case in the given situation.

SUMMARY

In this chapter, we have provided some of the basics, especially as they relate to organizing and delivering the speech. Each speech has an introduction, a body, and a conclusion. Within that structure, there are methods for organizing a speech for informing or persuading. The extemporaneous delivery system is recommended for most public speeches. The next few chapters provide more detail about how to organize and collect materials so that you will be fully prepared.

At this point, we have discussed briefly the primary points in delivering a quality speech. The remaining chapters are more detailed versions of organizing speeches, researching for speeches, and delivering speeches. Even now, though, you should be able to speak on some topic about which you have a great deal of information. For example, you should be able to deliver a talk about who you are, what you want to do when you graduate, the values of coming from a small town (or a big city), your favorite hobby, and the like. The next two chapters deal with the concept of fear in public speaking. Chapter 3 is about analyzing your apprehension. Chapter 4 is about overcoming those fears.

3 Scared Speechless

Most people have a strong desire to be perceived as competent communicators. Exactly what it takes to be an effective, competent communicator has been discussed for hundreds of years. In fact, the oldest essay ever discovered, written about 3000 B.C., consisted of advice on how to speak effectively. With hundreds of years and thousands of writings on how to be a competent, effective speaker, you might think we would know what it takes to be an effective communicator (Richmond & McCroskey, 1998). We can narrow it down to at least four primary problems a speaker must overcome to be effective.

Poor Cognitive, Affective, and Behavioral Orientations (CABs)

CABs are the cognitive, affective, and behavioral orientations toward communication. *Cognitive skills* are central in becoming a truly effective communicator. Such skills involve understanding and comprehending the communication process and choosing appropriate content to communicate and content not to communicate to your audience. Many writers on public speaking give the cognitive little credit in the communication process. We, however, suggest that the cognitive, or knowing about communication, can determine your success or failure. Just as in so many other learning situations, using your brain can help! In the communication process, using your brain to understand your audience members, comprehend what they want or need to hear, and decide how to present it is critical in your success as a competent and effective communicator. This book makes a concerted effort to add to your brain power in the area of public presentation.

Affective orientations toward communication, our feelings and emotions, can influence our competence as a communicator. "All of the behavioral and cognitive skills in the world will not make a person an effective communicator if they do not want to be one" (Richmond & McCroskey, 1998, p. 3). There must be a desire to communicate; to present yourself well; to influence, inform, or have simple conversation. If desire and motivation are absent, then effective communication will not be present. If doing math is not a skill you feel you need, then you may put little effort into learning math skills. The same is true for communication. The desire to communicate must be coupled with cognitive and behavioral skills. Therefore, if you perceive yourself to be low in communication competence, then you may not be perceived as a competent communicator. Now complete the Self-Perceived Communication Competence (SPCC) scale provided in Table 3.1. Once you have your score, you will know how you feel about your self-perceived communication competence. High self-perceived communication competence correlates positively with higher self-esteem, willingness to communicate, and a generally positive attitude toward communication. Low competence is associated with communication apprehension, shyness, and introversion. Therefore, the higher your SPCC score (the more competent you think you are), the higher your positive affect for communication.

Behavioral skills make it possible to be effective communicators. Certain verbal and nonverbal communication skills are essential to effective communication. Such variables as language, body movements, eye contact with listeners, good articulation, overcoming speech problems, and not appearing shy are a few of the significant skills needed. With brain power, effort, and the motivation to speak, all of the above skills can be learned and used in the appropriate situation.

When people do not use their brains, they may not be effective communicators. In fact, others might perceive them as incompetent. When they do not care to communicate well, then others might perceive them as incompetent. When they do not display the appropriate communication behavioral skills, then others might perceive them as incompetent.

Shyness

In our culture the attitude toward talking is "talk more, not less." An enormous number of studies have confirmed that talking more carries more positive perceptions and rewards than talking less in this culture. Being shy is a primary reason why people talk less. Being shy is another reason why people would perceive someone to be an incompetent communicator. Being shy prevents one from talking. Because shyness makes it difficult to communicate, a shy person does not get as much practice at communicating as does one who is not shy. Shyness can get in the way of competent communication. Complete the Shyness Scale (SS) in Table 3.2 to determine your shyness.

Shyness refers to a person's behavioral tendency not to talk (McCroskey & Richmond, 1996; Richmond & McCroskey, 1998). The best method for determining your shyness level is the Shyness Scale. The

TABLE 3.1 Self-Perceived Communication Competence (SPCC)

Directions: Below are twelve situations in which you might need to communicate. Indicate how competent you believe you are to communicate in each of these situations. Indicate in the space at the left of each item your estimate of your competence. Presume 0 = completely incompetent and 100 = competent.

_94_	**1.**	Present a talk to a group of strangers
_92_	**2.**	Talk with an acquaintance
_87_	**3.**	Talk in a large meeting with friends
_90_	**4.**	Talk in a small group of strangers
_99_	**5.**	Talk with a friend
_85_	**6.**	Talk in a large meeting of acquaintances
_98_	**7.**	Talk with a stranger
_90_	**8.**	Present a talk to a group of friends
_86_	**9.**	Talk in a small group of acquaintances
_85_	**10.**	Talk in a large meeting of strangers
_94_	**11.**	Talk in a small group of friends
_90_	**12.**	Present a talk to a group of acquaintances

Scoring

To compute the subscores, add the percentages for the items indicated and divide the total by the number indicated below.

91	Public	1 + 8 + 12; divide by 3	>86 High SPCC <51 Low SPCC
85	Meeting	3 + 6 + 10; divide by 3	>85 High SPCC <51 Low SPCC
90	Group	4 + 9 + 11; divide by 3	>90 High SPCC <61 Low SPCC
96	Dyad	2 + 5 + 7; divide by 3	>93 High SPCC <68 Low SPCC
91	Stranger	1 + 4 + 7 + 10; divide by 4	>79 High SPCC <31 Low SPCC
89	Acquaintance	2 + 6 + 9 + 12; divide by 4	>99 High SPCC <62 Low SPCC
92	Friend	3 + 5 + 8 + 11; divide by 4	>87 High SPCC <76 Low SPCC
	TOTAL SPCC 90.6		>87 High SPCC <59 Low SPCC

To compute the total SPCC score, add the subscores for Stranger, Acquaintance, and Friend. Then divide that total by 3.

Higher SPCC scores indicate high self-perceived communication competence with basic communication contexts (public, meeting, group, dyad) and receivers (strangers, acquaintances, friend).

Source: From V. P. Richmond & J. C. McCroskey, *Communication: Apprehension, avoidance, and effectiveness.* © 1998. Reprinted by permission by Allyn & Bacon.

TABLE 3.2   Shyness Scale (SS)

Directions: The following fourteen statements refer to talking with other people.

If a statement describes you well, circle a 5.
If a statement is a somewhat good description of you, circle a 4.
If you are undecided or unsure if a statement represents you, circle a 3.
If a statement is a somewhat poor description of you, circle a 2.
If a statement is a very poor description of you, circle a 1.

Work quickly; record your first impressions.

1. I am a shy person.   5 4 3 (2) 1
2. Other people think I talk a lot.   5 4 (3) 2 1
3. I am a very talkative person.   5 4 (3) 2 1
4. Other people think I am shy.   5 4 (3) 2 1
5. I talk a lot.   5 4 3 (2) 1
6. I tend to be very quiet in class.   (5) 4 3 2 1
7. I don't talk much.   5 4 3 (2) 1
8. I talk more than most people.   5 4 (3) 2 1
9. I am a quiet person.   5 4 3 (2) 1
10. I talk more in a small group (3 to 6) than others do.   5 (4) 3 2 1
11. Most people talk more than I do.   5 (4) 3 2 1
12. Other people think I am very quiet.   5 4 (3) 2 1
13. I talk more in class than most people do.   5 4 3 (2) 1
14. Most people are more shy than I am.   5 4 (3) 2 1

Scoring

Step 1: Add the scores for items 1, 4, 6, 7, 9, 11, and 12. 21
Step 2: Add the scores for items 2, 3, 5, 8, 10, 13, and 14. 20
Step 3: Complete the following formula: Shyness = 42 + Total from Step 2 – Total from Step 1. = 41

Your score should be between 14 and 120.
Scores above 52 indicate a high level of shyness.
Scores below 32 indicate a low level of shyness.
Scores between 32 and 52 indicate a moderate level of shyness.

Source: From V. P. Richmond & J. C. McCroskey, *Communication: Apprehension, avoidance, and effectiveness.* © 1998. Reprinted by permission by Allyn & Bacon.

best way others can determine if you are shy is by watching you not communicate. Shy people demonstrate they are shy by not communicating. Their primary behavior is one of not talking. There are five types of shyness: (1) the skill deficient, (2) the socially introverted, (3) the culturally introverted, (4) the socially alienated, and (5) the ethnically/culturally divergent.

Skill Deficient

Lacking behavioral skills to communicate effectively can lead to the behavior of not talking or communicating. Most communication skill–deficient people consciously or unconsciously learn to avoid communication situations. After behaving this way for a long period of time, the behavior of not communicating becomes a pattern. If people do not believe they possess the skills to communicate, then often they will not communicate. The few who are shy and try to communicate before building up their communication skills often fail at communication or look as if they are trying too hard to communicate. Skill-deficient people in most areas avoid situations that call for those skills. For example, if you have poor computer skills, you probably avoid using a computer in front of other more skilled computer users.

Socially Introverted

Some people have a high need and desire to be with others. They are called social extroverts. Some have a high need and desire to be alone most of the time. These people are referred to as social introverts. Literally, social introverts prefer their own company to the company of friends or large numbers of other people. Extroverts are outgoing, are amiable, and often are real talkers. Introverts are distant, aloof, and often not real talkers. Think about this example: Have you ever seen or met an introverted politician? Probably not. Politicians must be outgoing to get votes and to get their message to their constituents. It is an oxymoron to be a shy politician.

Culturally Introverted

People of some cultures, such as parts of Scandinavia and Asia, are more introverted than people in the United States, Latin America, or southern Europe. In some cultures quietness is a virtue. That is not true for our culture. Being quiet in North America often gets you labeled as shy, quiet, reclusive, unfriendly, and incompetent. Whereas being quiet may be the norm for some cultures, it is not the norm in North America.

Socially Alienated

Most people in the culture of the United States attempt to fit in or be compatible with cultural expectations. This behavior is considered the behavior of a well-adjusted person. Those who reject the cultural norms or act in opposition to the cultural norms are often isolated from others and from society as a whole. Therefore, those who become socially alienated may not get the opportunity to practice their communication skills. Then they may avoid many communication situations. Remember those early years in school when you wanted to fit in. If you did not fit in then, you may have felt rejected or isolated. Because of this rejection and isolation perhaps you did not learn as many communication skills for a variety of situations as did those people who fit in.

Ethnically/Culturally Divergent

Even all citizens of the United States are different from one another. In fact, most people have had the experience of being both in the majority and in the minority at one time or another. Being different, ethnically or culturally, means people are in the minority and might be unable to cope fully with the new communication demands they confront. Therefore, they behave as if they are shy. For example, someone from South Los Angeles who visits a friend in Kansas (or vice versa) might be in the minority. This feeling of being in the minority can cause people to behave in a shy manner.

Thus, one who is skill deficient, socially introverted, culturally introverted, alienated, or ethnically/culturally divergent may experience shyness and engage in the behavior of not communicating. Another reason for shy behavior can be communication apprehension (CA).

Communication Apprehension (CA)

Communication apprehension (CA) is a fear or an anxiety associated with real or anticipated communication with another person or persons (McCroskey, 1997). By far one of the largest groups of quiet or shy people are those who are apprehensive. High CA people recognize the need to communicate and have the desire to communicate, but they are blocked or inhibited by their fear or anxiety. They "choke" or become unnaturally anxious when asked to communicate. Complete the Personal Report of Communication Apprehension 24 (PRCA 24) in Table 3.3 to get your overall CA score and a score for group discussion, meetings, conversation, and public speaking. For most persons in the culture of the United States, their highest score will be in the public speaking arena. Occasionally, a few are unusually high on the conversation CA but low on the public speaking CA. In many organizations workers are often more apprehensive when it comes to meetings. This apprehension about meetings is usually explained as "where we are expected to give public presentations" or "this is a high evaluation situation." Studies suggest that 20 percent of the population, or one in five persons, suffers from high CA. Remember that not all quiet people are high CA, but most high CA people are quiet. Therefore, quiet people are often seen as shy people. The highly apprehensive person fears or becomes anxious about communication, and one means of coping with this fear may be to avoid communication or not to talk. Communication-apprehensive persons differ from other quiet or shy people in two very important ways: They tend to have low self-esteem and a low level of willingness to communicate. Highly apprehensive people do not differ substantially from low-apprehensive persons in intelligence. There are as many smart high CA people as there are smart low CA people. Also, there are as many less-than-bright low CA people as there are less-than-bright high CA people (Richmond & McCroskey, 1998).

Willingness to Communicate (WTC)

Willingness to communicate (WTC) refers to the person's level of desire to initiate and respond to communication with others (McCroskey & Richmond, 1996). A person with high willingness to communicate has a higher desire to initiate and respond to communication with others. On the other hand, a person with low willingness to communicate has a lower desire to initiate and respond to communication with others. There is a strong relationship between CA and WTC. An individual's level of CA probably is the single best predictor of a person's willingness to communicate. Complete the willingness to communicate (WTC) measure in

TABLE 3.3   Personal Report of Communication Apprehension 24 (PRCA 24)

Directions: This instrument is composed of twenty-four statements concerning feelings about communicating with other people. Indicate in the space at the left of each item the degree to which the statement applies to you.

> 1 = Strongly Agree
> 2 = Agree
> 3 = Undecided or Unsure
> 4 = Disagree
> 5 = Strongly Disagree

_____ 1. I dislike participating in group discussions.

_____ 2. Generally, I am comfortable while participating in group discussions.

_____ 3. I am tense and nervous while participating in group discussions.

_____ 4. I like to get involved in group discussions.

_____ 5. Engaging in a group discussion with new people makes me tense and nervous.

_____ 6. I am calm and relaxed while participating in group discussions.

_____ 7. Generally, I am nervous when I have to participate in meetings.

_____ 8. Usually, I am calm and relaxed while participating in meetings.

_____ 9. I am very calm and relaxed when I am called upon to express an opinion at a meeting.

_____ 10. I am afraid to express myself at meetings.

_____ 11. Communicating at meetings usually makes me uncomfortable.

_____ 12. I am very relaxed when answering questions at a meeting.

_____ 13. While participating in a conversation with a new acquaintance, I feel very nervous.

_____ 14. I have no fear of speaking up in conversations.

_____ 15. Ordinarily, I am very tense and nervous in conversations.

_____ 16. While conversing with a new acquaintance, I feel very relaxed.

_____ 17. Ordinarily, I am very tense and nervous in conversations.

_____ 18. I am afraid to speak up in conversations.

_____ 19. I have no fear of giving a speech.

_____ 20. Certain parts of my body feel very tense and rigid while I am giving a speech.

(continued)

TABLE 3.3   Continued

_____ **21.** I feel relaxed while giving a speech.

_____ **22.** My thoughts become confused and jumbled when I am giving a speech.

_____ **23.** I face the prospect of giving a speech with confidence.

_____ **24.** While giving a speech, I get so nervous I forget facts I really know.

Scoring

Step 1: Add the scores for items 2, 4, 6, 8, 9, 12, 14, 16, 19, 21, and 23.
Step 2: Add the scores for items 1, 3, 5, 7, 10, 11, 13, 15, 17, 18, 20, 22, and 24.
Step 3: Add 72 to the score in Step 1.
Step 4: Subtract the score for Step 2 from the score for Step 3.

Scores above 80 = High CA.
Scores below 50 = Low CA.

Source: From V. P. Richmond & J. C. McCroskey, _Communication: Apprehension, avoidance, and effectiveness._ © 1998. Reprinted by permission by Allyn & Bacon.

Table 3.4 and compare your overall score with your overall CA score. Then compare your WTC scores on groups, meetings, conversation, and public speaking with your CA scores on groups, meetings, conversation, or public speaking. On the WTC you can also get scores for speaking with certain receivers—strangers, acquaintances, and friends.

Communication apprehension, then, is what you may feel when communicating. You feel anxious, fearful, or scared speechless. Willingness to communicate is your general inclination toward talk, and shyness is the degree to which you actually avoid talking. Subsequently, people might refer to you as shy or quiet.

Although not everyone who is quiet is alike, the impact of their quietness tends to be about the same. Not all quiet people are high communication apprehensives, but many are. Not all people who are quiet are unwilling to communicate, but many are. Not all people who are quiet are shy, but many are (Richmond & McCroskey, 1998, p. 38).

Shyness, CA, and WTC are more _trait-like_ orientations. This means that there is little difference regardless of the context. In the next section, we review several situational factors that impact fear of communicating with others.

TABLE 3.4   Willingness to Communicate (WTC) Measure

Directions: Below are twenty situations in which a person might choose to communicate or not to communicate. Presume you have *completely free choice.* Determine the percentage of times you would choose to initiate communication in each type of situation. Indicate in the space at the left of each item what percent of the time you would choose to communicate. Select a percentage for each individual item between 0 percent and 100 percent.

_____   **1.** Talk with a service station attendant

_____   **2.** Talk with a physician

_____   **3.** Present a talk to a group of strangers

_____   **4.** Talk with an acquaintance while standing in line

_____   **5.** Talk with a salesperson in a store

_____   **6.** Talk in a large meeting of friends

_____   **7.** Talk with a police officer

_____   **8.** Talk in a small group of strangers

_____   **9.** Talk with a friend while standing in line

_____   **10.** Talk with a waiter/waitress in a restaurant

_____   **11.** Talk in a large meeting of acquaintances

_____   **12.** Talk with a stranger while standing in line

_____   **13.** Talk with a secretary

_____   **14.** Present a talk to a group of friends

_____   **15.** Talk in a small group of acquaintances

_____   **16.** Talk with a garbage collector

_____   **17.** Talk in a large meeting of strangers

_____   **18.** Talk with a spouse (or girl/boyfriend)

_____   **19.** Talk in a small group of friends

_____   **20.** Present a talk to a group of acquaintances

Scoring

Step 1: Add the scores for items 3, 4, 6, 8, 9, 11, 12, 14, 15, 17, 19, and 20.
Step 2: Divide the score from Step 1 by 12.

Scores above 80 = High WTC.

Scores below 52 = Low WTC.

Source: From V. P. Richmond & J. C. McCroskey, *Communication: Apprehension, avoidance, and effectiveness.* © 1998. Reprinted by permission by Allyn & Bacon.

The Big Nine Situational Causes

The causes of *situational CA* are numerous and can vary from one situation to another. The situational factors that impact communication apprehension are novelty, formality, subordinate status, conspicuousness, unfamiliarity, dissimilarity, degree of attention/excessive attention from others, degree of evaluation, and prior communication history (Richmond & McCroskey, 1998).

Novelty.   Most people become situationally anxious or nervous when they encounter a new, different, or novel situation. For example, meeting a new business associate might cause some situational anxiety as might going for an interview. Such novel communication situations can cause us to experience some temporary anxiety.

Formality.   In formal situations there is often little latitude for communication errors. Therefore, in more formal situations people might experience some anxiety. Attending a formal wedding, banquet, graduation, or business reception at which a particular communication protocol is expected can cause us to become anxious.

Subordinate Status.   This occurs when one person has higher status than another. When you are the subordinate, you may not know what, when, or how to communicate with your superior. Therefore, you may experience situational anxiety.

Conspicuousness.   Being conspicuous, noticeable, prominent, or standing out can cause you to feel anxiety. For example, wearing incorrect clothing to a formal presentation could cause a conspicuous feeling. Having broccoli stuck between your front teeth and knowing it is there could cause a feeling of conspicuousness.

Unfamiliarity.   The less familiar you are with a certain situation, the more anxious you might be about your communication. Traveling from one culture to another can give a sense of unfamiliarity, therefore creating situational communication anxiety.

Dissimilarity.   The more dissimilar you feel from others, the more difficulty you have communicating with them. As dissimilarity increases, so does anxiety. You get the chance of a lifetime to meet your favorite movie or music star, but because of the dissimilarity to that person you feel great discomfort or anxiety.

Degree of Attention.   Most people like some attention from others, but many do not want to be the center of attention. When they become the center of attention or get "put on the spot," they may become situationally anxious. Being asked spontaneously to toast another person's achievement may direct unusual and unwanted attention on them, thus causing situational anxiety.

Degree of Evaluation.   The more people feel they are being evaluated or judged, the more likely their situational anxiety is to increase. When presenting a paper before a class of our peers we might experience situational anxiety.

Prior History.   If you have a prior communication history of failure with a certain group or person, then your anxiety may increase. If your prior history is good with a certain group of persons, then your anxiety may not increase. For example, if talking with your girl- or boyfriend's parents or your in-laws has never been a good experience and you seem to say the wrong things, then your situational anxiety will increase if you have to do it again.

In conclusion, situational communication anxiety can be caused by a number of factors or one factor. The factors that cause situational communication anxiety can vary from one person to the next. Perhaps you are more anxious when the situation is novel and your friend is more anxious when feeling evaluated.

SUMMARY

Poor cognitive, affective, and behavioral orientations toward communication cause a speaker to be a less effective communicator. As well, shyness and communication apprehension have a negative effect on being a good speaker. In addition, a low willingness to communicate is obvious to listeners, who may have a less than positive view of your communication. All of these factors are trait factors—they occur across situations. There are other cases in which effective talk is damaged by situational factors, including the novelty of the situation, the formality of the situation, having a subordinate status, appearing conspicuous, unfamiliarity with the situation, being dissimilar from others, receiving undue attention, being judged, and having a prior history with a situation. In any case, a speaker needs to work on those areas in which he or she is less effective. In this chapter, we presented some of the causes. The next chapter focuses on potential solutions.

EXERCISE

Everyone has learned various methods of coping with situational communication apprehension. Below, list at least two ways you cope effectively with the following situations:

Situation	*Cope with the Situation*
Novel	
Formal	
Subordinate status	
Conspicuousness	
Unfamiliarity	
Dissimilarity	
Attention from others	
Degree of evaluation	
Prior history	

4 Fighting the Fear

When most people are asked to present a speech, they immediately become anxious, fearful, or even terrified. They may experience dry mouth; queasy stomach; urination urges; the shakes and fidgets; chest pains; wet, sweaty palms; and a brain that does not seem to be working the way it should. For those who are not generally apprehensive or anxious, they may experience these physiological side effects only when speaking before a particular person or group or in a novel, unfamiliar situation. For those with generally high anxiety/fear, these symptoms will be present the majority of the time.

Fear not! You are not alone with this speech anxiety dilemma. Even some superstars in the entertainment business have expressed being fearful in certain speaking situations. It is suggested that even Abraham Lincoln and Mark Twain were highly apprehensive about speaking. This chapter reviews how to assist generally highly apprehensive/fearful people fight the fear. We cannot promise an overnight cure but can give you methods to help manage some of your anxiety.

Myths about Fighting Fear

Look at the Imaginary Dot on the Back Wall Right above the Audience's Heads.   This is nonsense! Not only does this not reduce fear and apprehension, it annoys the audience because they cannot have eye contact with you. A good colleague of ours speaks like this at conventions, conferences, and other formal speaking sessions. Most audience members like him but are bothered by the lack of eye contact. The audience knows he is looking past and over their heads at some imaginary dot on the back wall. Remember that it is not good to annoy your audience.

Imagine Your Audience in Their Underwear or Naked.   This too is nonsense. First, to try to create this image interferes with your cognitive processing of the material you are to present. Second, if you can really imagine your audience in their underwear or naked, you may feel ill or begin laughing. Third, your facial expressions might give away what you are thinking. Fourth, you also will annoy the audience by not having normal, regular eye contact with them. Remember that it is not good to annoy your audience.

Be the First or Last Speaker.   This too is nonsense. If you are the first speaker, you have no way to adapt based on the other speakers. If you are the last speaker, you have compared yourself to all the other presenters. By this time, you are scared speechless and have convinced yourself that your speech will be awful. There really is no good time to present if you are anxious. Follow a good presenter and you are more scared. Be first and you are more conspicuous and the center of attention.

Medicate Yourself.   This too is nonsense and dangerous to your reputation. Whenever anyone suggests that you have a drink or two, that taking a pill or two will help, you should sue him or her for "friendship malpractice." Drinking or taking pills or both will not help you be a better presenter. It only makes you think you will be a better presenter and the presentation itself may be less painful, but the results can be devastating. Others will know you are not yourself, that you are medicated, and this can truly hurt your reputation.

Practice Makes Perfect.   Unfortunately for the people who are truly scared speechless, practice makes permanent, not necessarily perfect. We are not suggesting not to practice your presentation; we are saying practicing does not necessarily relieve generalized speech anxiety. Practice is very good for anyone presenting but it should never be used as a cure for speech anxiety.

Helping, Not Hurting

Now that we have established five myths about reducing fear or anxiety, let us move to methods for decreasing communication apprehension or the fear of speaking. The next section reviews how to help with excessive activation, inappropriate cognitive processing, and inadequate communication skills.

Excessive Activation

Any person can remember the first time he or she was expected to speak in front of others, got to drive a car, performed on stage, played center field, attended a formal dinner and dance, passionately kissed another person, or was introduced to a really important person. Some felt excited, fearful, or had stomachaches, headaches, or neck aches. This is often referred to by athletes as "getting psyched." This increase in the physiological activation in your body is normal. In fact, such an increase in activation often is essential to a quality performance.

Excessive activation is altogether different from getting psyched. Excessive activation usually is not good for us. It is a physiological overreaction to an upcoming performance that can keep people from performing normally. Several methods of reducing excessive activation include hypnotism, meditation, biofeedback, use of certain prescribed medications, and deep muscular relaxation techniques. The relaxation techniques have been more successful than the other methods. Deep muscular relaxation as a part of "systematic desensitization" has been proven quite successful in treating many phobias, such as speaking anxiety. This is reviewed in more depth later in this chapter.

Inappropriate Cognitive Processing

This is thinking the wrong way. Often the fear of speaking is in the mind, not the body. True, the body may demonstrate the fear but the fear starts in the mind. People need to learn to relax. With inappropriate cognitive processing, they need to learn to rethink or reprocess cognitive ideas. A behavior therapy known as "cognitive restructuring" is known to assist in changing a person's mind about speaking. Cognitive restructuring was developed to overcome communication anxiety in addition to other phobic anxieties. Some people simply cope better than others with communication anxiety. Some people can cognitively process information to their advantage; others cannot. Those who are highly aroused mentally in a negative way (feel sick) need to cognitively restructure how they think about speaking situations. Cognitive restructuring is reviewed in more depth later in the chapter.

Inadequate Communication Skills

When people are deficient in any skill, they usually become anxious. Therefore, when a presenter is deficient in public presentation skills, he or she may be reluctant to perform. This is perfectly normal. If a person does not know how to do something, but is forced to do it anyway, to be fearful or anxious is a normal reaction. For example, if you do not know how to cook and prepare meals but must do so for a birthday party for your significant other, your feelings are normal. Fortunately, you can order prepared food for the birthday party. Most people cannot order other persons to give their speech presentations for them.

If you cannot present well because you are skill deficient, then this book provides ideas, methods, and training to help improve your performance skills. If you cannot present well because of cognitive fear or excessive activation, then you need some systematic desensitization (deep muscular relaxation) or cognitive restructuring (thinking differently) or both prior to your performance. The next section of this text reviews the most commonly employed methods for treating communication or performance anxiety.

Relax and Learn to Communicate Fearlessly

Deep Muscular Relaxation

Systematic desensitization (SD) is a behavior therapy originally developed by Wolpe (1958). It has been used extensively by psychologists, psychiatrists, and public performance experts to reduce apprehension. In this field, SD is often used to help alleviate fear of speaking. SD is very successful in reducing students' apprehension about public presentation. Let us keep in mind that this method works for approximately 80 percent of highly fearful people. We have made the deep muscular relaxation or SD manageable because you may not have a program in your area. Therefore, what we are presenting is a modified version of SD. To conduct SD successfully, two components must be in place:

1. Learning the procedures for deep muscular relaxation.
2. Visualizing yourself participating in a series of communication situations while in a state of deep relaxation. The series is ordered from the least anxiety-provoking situation (talking to your best friend) to the most anxiety-provoking situation (you are to appear on a television show and cannot find your notes).

SD can be administered either on an individual basis or in a small group of normally five to seven people. A typical program includes five to seven one-hour sessions spread over several days or weeks. The following steps will enable you to administer deep muscular relaxation and visualization.

Step 1: Make yourself comfortable.   You should be seated in a comfortable chair; lean back and relax. Select an area where you will not be disturbed by phone, fax, people, and so on. Give yourself an hour in this quiet, comfortable area.

Step 2: Once you are comfortable and assured that nothing will disturb you, turn on a prerecorded tape that includes instructions for deep muscular relaxation.   This tape instructs you to tense and relax each of the major muscle groups in the body. The total time for this deep muscular relaxation process is about twenty-five minutes. (An example of the relaxation exercises is provided in Table 4.1.)

Step 3: When the instructions for relaxation have been completed, turn off the recorder.   You should have your recorder or another piece of equipment make a small sound at the end of the tape. This is necessary because in a state of deep relaxation people tend to fall asleep. Start visualizing yourself in the least threatening communication situation, such as "You are talking to your best friend." (Examples of nonthreatening to threatening communication situations are provided in Table 4.2). Remain silent for approximately fifteen seconds while watching for indications of tension. If your body signals tension, then you should put the situation out of your mind and then provide a few moments of relaxation instruction similar to those on the prerecorded tape. If you feel no tension for fifteen seconds, put the situation out of your mind and provide a few moments of relaxation instructions before visualizing the situation again.

Step 4: If you feel any tension, the process of visualization is continuously repeated, until you feel no tension for fifteen seconds.   Then, after a few moments of relaxation instructions, the visualization is repeated with you waiting thirty seconds before terminating the visualization unless your body signals that it is experiencing tension. If there is such a signal, the same procedure used with the fifteen-second interval is employed. The process is repeated until you can visualize the situation for fifteen and thirty seconds sequentially without experiencing tension.

* This tape can be purchased as part of this course from the National Communication Association.

TABLE 4.1   **Examples of Muscle Relaxation**

Based on the work of Wolpe (1958), systematic desensitization is a treatment program that includes (1) training in deep muscular relaxation; (2) a hierarchy of anxiety-eliciting stimuli; and (3) the pairing, through imagery, of the anxiety-producing stimuli on the hierarchy with relaxation. Using Jacobson's (1938) progressive muscle relaxation training, the following muscle groups are tensed for several seconds, then relaxed. Mental note is made of how good the relaxation feels.

Again, much repetition might take place in each muscle group to become totally relaxed. Usually, each group is tensed and relaxed at least twice before moving on to the next muscle group. A common range is five to ten seconds for tensing a muscle and ten to fifteen seconds for relaxation.

1. Hands (Clench and unclench right hand, then left hand.)
2. Biceps and triceps (Bend right hand upward at wrist, pointing fingers toward ceiling, relax, then left hand; bring both hands up toward shoulders, flex biceps, then relax; repeat.)
3. Shoulders (Shrug shoulders, hold, relax.)
4. Neck (Push head against chair, relax; lean forward, relax.)
5. Mouth (Press lips tightly together, then relax.)
6. Tongue (Extend, hold, retract.)
7. Tongue (Press mouth roof, relax; press mouth floor, relax.)
8. Eyes and forehead (Close eyes tightly, relax; wrinkle forehead, relax.)
9. Breathing (Inhale, hold, exhale.)
10. Back (Arch back, hold, relax.)
11. Midsection (Tense muscles including buttocks, hold, relax.)
12. Thighs (Tense muscles, hold, relax.)
13. Stomach (Suck in stomach, hold, relax.)
14. Calves and feet (Stretch out both legs, hold, relax.)
15. Toes (Point toes toward ceiling, hold, relax; point toes downward, hold, relax.)

TABLE 4.2   Samples of Nonthreatening to Threatening Communication Situations

(*Note:* The entire hierarchy can be built around a single fear or situation.)

1. You are talking to your best friend on the phone.
2. You are talking to your best friend in person.
3. You are being introduced to a new acquaintance by your best friend.
4. You are having to introduce yourself to a new acquaintance.
5. You are talking to an operator about placing a long-distance phone call.
6. You are talking to a salesperson in a department store.
7. You have to talk to a small group of people, all of whom you know well.
8. You are talking to a supervisor or someone who is in a supervisory role, such as a teacher, about a problem at work or school.
9. You are at a social gathering where you don't know anyone, but are expected to meet and talk to others.
10. You are going to ask someone to go to a movie with you.
11. You are going to ask someone to go to a social gathering with you.
12. You have to talk to a police officer about a ticket.
13. You are going on a job interview.
14. You have been asked to give a presentation in front of a large group of people.
15. You are getting ready to give a public speech but realize you left your notes at home.
16. You are to appear on a panel television show with others and talk about a topic you know well.
17. You are to appear on a television show and debate another person.
18. You are ready to appear on a television show and give a speech but you lost your notes.

Step 5: At this point you should move on to the second communication situation and repeat exactly the procedure used with the first communication situation.   This process is continued until all of the communication situations have been successfully visualized without tension or until the time to end the session is near. If the number of situations to which you are to be exposed is typical (sixteen to eighteen), the entire list will not be completed in the first session, nor likely even in the first four or five sessions.

Step 6: To complete a given session, you should visualize a situation you have already successfully visualized without tension for approximately sixty seconds.   This will help ensure that you are still deeply relaxed as the session ends. At this point you should open your eyes and gradually become reacquainted with your surroundings. After you have become more alert, practice the relaxation exercises daily in between sessions and try to use them to become relaxed if you confront stressful communication situations during the intervening time period.

Step 7: In subsequent sessions the same procedures are followed as in the first session with only minor variations.   In later sessions it might be unnecessary to play the entire tape of relaxation instructions. This is particularly true if you have been given a copy of the tape in order to practice between sessions. Also in later sessions you might begin with somewhat more stressful communication situations than the original one, but avoid starting with any situation that prompted tension in the preceding session. After two or three sessions you should review your outside experiences in attempting to use the learned techniques in real communication situations. This helps to reinforce that you should be making such attempts.

Ideally, sessions should continue until you can visualize all of the communication situations without experiencing tension. If this is accomplished before the scheduled number of sessions has been held (normally five to seven), the program can be terminated early. If this has not been accomplished when the last scheduled session is completed, additional sessions should be added. If you seem to be reacting with significantly more tension, you may need to complete more sessions. This occurs relatively rarely because the treatment is so highly effective; however, there are a few people who are not helped by the method and who continue to respond with very high tension during the treatment sessions. For this small percentage, one of the other methods described should be substituted.

Systematic desensitization is an extremely effective method for helping people overcome fear of speaking or stage fright. Research indicates approximately 90 percent of the people who receive this treatment reduce their fear of communication, and of those who enter the treatment as highly communication apprehensive, 80 percent are no longer high apprehensive after treatment.

As noted earlier, systematic desensitization is the most appropriate method of treating communication apprehension if one presumes the problem stems from excessive physiological activation. McCroskey, Ralph, and Barrick (1970) tested to determine the effects of this method on such activation. They found that measured heart rate activation in participants reporting high anxiety greatly increased as they were exposed to a formal communication situation prior to treatment. After treatment, however, these same participants could control their activation so that no similar increase occurred.

The effectiveness of systematic desensitization is not restricted to simply increasing control of activation. A number of studies have found cognitive effects in terms of substantially reduced scores on the Personal Report of Communication Apprehension. In addition, Goss, Thompson, and Olds (1978) reported meaningful improvements in communication behavior. Although the exact reason why systematic desensitization works remains a subject of scholarly dispute, that it works, and works well, is clearly established.

Cognitive Restructuring

The method of *cognitive restructuring* (Meichenbaum, 1977) evolved from an earlier method known as rational-emotive therapy (Ellis, 1962). Both are based on the following:

1. The idea that you have irrational thoughts about yourself and your behaviors
2. That these thoughts increase the anxiety you are likely to have about situations such as communicating with others

In rational-emotive therapy the persons receiving treatment are encouraged to identify irrational beliefs they have about communication. Then these beliefs are attacked logically in an attempt to demonstrate to the individuals that they should change their ways of thinking. The assumption is that if the irrational thoughts are eliminated, the apprehension will be reduced.

The cognitive restructuring approach goes one step further. In addition to identifying the illogical beliefs the person holds, he or she must formulate new, more appropriate beliefs. This method recognizes that simple elimination of illogical beliefs might not be enough and that the replacement of displaced beliefs by more appropriate beliefs is an important positive step.

Like systematic desensitization, cognitive restructuring typically is administered in five or six one-hour sessions spread over several days or weeks. Treatment might be administered to people on an individual basis or in small groups of typically four to eight people. As outlined by Fremouw and Scott (1979), the treatment involves four steps:

> Step 1: Introduction of the person being treated to the method
>
> Step 2: Identification of negative self-statements (illogical beliefs)
>
> Step 3: Learning coping statements (beliefs to replace the illogical ones)
>
> Step 4: Practice

First Session.   During the first session you should learn the following:

1. You need to understand that apprehension or fear of communication is a learned reaction that most people can change in a few hours.
2. Remind yourself that people mentally talk to themselves and that the self-statements they make might be completely irrational and harmful.
3. Finally, by learning positive coping statements to substitute for the harmful ones, you can reduce your apprehension or fear of speaking.

Following these ideas, you are encouraged to identify specific negative self-statements or thoughts that increase your apprehension. You should provide a large number of examples to illustrate the kind of statement under consideration; for instance, "I will throw up if I have to give a speech," "This interview is the most important thing in my life," "No one will like me if I don't do well," and "I don't know how to ask for a date." After you understand what negative self-statements you use, identify and write down three or four that you commonly make to yourself. Review these statements in terms of how they might affect your feelings about communication. Logical errors ("If everyone does not agree with me, I have failed") and self-fulfilling prophecies ("I will do a miserable job") are pointed out also. At the conclusion of the first session, you are asked to continue to be aware of the negative self-statements you use regarding communication. Again, you are encouraged to write down these statements and have them for your second session.

Second Session.   This session begins with a review of the negative self-statements that you make and examples of statements you have used since the previous session. This is handled in much the same way as were the negative self-statements in the first session. When this session is completed, you should work to generate positive self-statements (coping statements), that can be substituted for the negative ones. Different groups of statements are generated for use before, during, and after the communication event. Examples of such statements might be "Most of these people really want to hear my ideas," "This really is quite easy," and "I did a good job." At the conclusion of this session, you are encouraged to attempt to substitute the positive self-statements for the negative ones when you are communicating with other people before your next session.

Subsequent Sessions.   The remaining sessions are devoted to guided practice in using the coping statements. You should review the topics of an increasingly controversial nature. Keep a diary identifying stressful communication situations you have experienced both within the treatment sessions and between sessions, describing the coping statements you used in those situations. When you can record that you have used coping statements in stressful communication situations, the practice sessions are terminated and the treatment program is complete.

Conclusions about Cognitive Restructuring.   Research involving cognitive restructuring indicates it is effective in accomplishing its specific objective—reducing self-reported apprehension about communication. Its effectiveness seems to be roughly equal to that of systematic desensitization in this regard. There is evidence that cognitive restructuring also reduces observable manifestations of anxiety in communication encounters.

Some treatment programs have been developed that include both systematic desensitization and cognitive restructuring methods. Research indicates that the two together are more effective than either is alone, but as yet there is insufficient data to be certain this is the case. Current research, however, suggests that SD should first be administered, then cognitive restructuring.

Skills Training

Unlike the two previously outlined treatment methods, which consist of generally accepted, formalized procedures, there are so many approaches to skills training it is difficult to outline what this method specifically includes or excludes. Programs labeled as "skills training" vary from a complete college course on communication skills to a few hours of training someone to go to an interview. Before we attempt to outline characteristics that a typical skills training program might include, we need to turn our attention to the general effectiveness of this approach.

We are familiar with the oldest and most widely used version of this treatment method: courses in speech or communication skills provided by high schools and colleges. In many instances these courses are required of all students in the school or in a given major. Survey research conducted with adults in the United States suggests this form of skills training is almost wholly ineffective in reducing general communication apprehension. Our respondents regularly indicate that the course either had no effect on their level of apprehension about communication or made it worse. However, skills training can be useful in helping people improve their public speaking skills, if, indeed, those skills are deficient. We are not suggesting that high schools and colleges that require speech courses are intentionally trying to damage the high CA; in fact, many of these programs are instituted to help shy people. The problem is that many times these programs do not help; they hurt. Therefore, alternative programs need to be offered to assist anxious or shy persons. Instead of a public presentation as the first requirement, have students talk with each other or complete other interpersonal or small group communication tasks. Shy persons can cope much easier with these tasks and learn not to fear communication even more.

In contrast, numerous studies involving skills training for such specific goals as increasing assertiveness, going for an interview, and learning to ask for a date have brought about major improvement in communication behavior, and at least a modest reduction in apprehension/fear about the specific type of communication addressed in the treatment. Notably, in almost all of this research the subjects volunteered for treatment and were not required to participate. They identified themselves as skill deficient in the treatment area.

We believe the differences in the effects of these two divergent types of skills training stem from two factors. The first is the need for the willing cooperation of the person being treated. The second relates to the need for skills training to have narrowly defined targets for improvement.

As noted previously, for any treatment program to be successful the recipient of the treatment must want to improve and be committed to the program. In the studies in which skills training has been found to be most effective, the volunteer participants had such a commitment. In contrast, data from our surveys of adults in the United States indicate that most of them took the speech or communication skills courses only because they were required to do so. The people who found the courses beneficial were primarily those who reported not having a high level of communication apprehension or fear to begin with. Of the relatively small number who said they did have a high level of communication apprehension and the course helped reduce it, virtually all had taken the course voluntarily. These results suggest, therefore, the skills training programs that do not allow students free choice to participate may cause students to become apprehensive or fearful. Public speaking is similar to swimming. In swimming, people learn not to fear the water and some beginning skills before they are expected to swim. Public speaking should follow the swimming learning model. In public speaking, speakers must learn not to fear the communication situation and develop some beginning skills before they can be expected to perform in public.

Another factor in distinguishing skills training programs relates to the definition of the target for improvement. Research in this area indicates the more narrowly the target behavior is defined, the greater the probability improvement will occur. In many skills-based courses the behaviors to be improved are very poorly defined. "To present an effective speech" or "to conduct an employment interview" are not unusual statements of objectives in such courses. These are much too broad to be specific training targets. Although these may be general goals of such courses, for skills training to be effective these broad behavioral goals must be broken down into specific behaviors that can be identified and learned.

Before we look at skills training as an approach in helping people to reduce communication apprehension, we need to make clear the primary purpose of skills training—to improve skills. Thus, a skills training program that can be demonstrated to improve skills should be judged successful, even if no impact on communication apprehension occurs at all. In some studies, this is the result that has been obtained. In others, some reduction in communication apprehension has also been observed.

Because skills training is time-consuming for both the professional helper and the person being treated, and thus tends to be expensive, its use as a method of helping people reduce communication apprehension should be restricted to instances in which a true communication skills deficit actually exists. It is not enough that the people who are to receive treatment think they are skill deficient; they must actually be so. If they are adequately skilled but think they are not, the problem is one of inappropriate cognitive processing, and cognitive restructuring should be the treatment of choice. If they have deficient skills but think their skills are satisfactory, no treatment is called for. Such individuals will lack the commitment to work with the professional helper, and consequently, no positive outcome is to be expected.

One final word of caution concerning the use of skills training. Improved skills can be expected to result only in areas in which specific skills training is provided. By this we mean that skills training does not generalize. As an illustration, consider skills training for public speaking. If specific training in how to construct a good introduction to a speech is provided, we should expect the person after training to be able to prepare a better introduction. However, we should not expect the person to be able to prepare a better conclusion or to prepare better for a formal interview.

An effective skills training program normally includes the following components:

1. Identifying the specific skill deficiency (or deficiencies)
2. Determining the subskills making up a larger area of deficient skill
3. Establishing attainable goals for acquiring new skills
4. Observing in an individual model the desirable skilled behavior to be learned
5. Developing a cognitive understanding of the nature of the skill to be learned (becoming able to explain verbally what is to be done)
6. Practicing the new behavior in a controlled, nonthreatening environment in which the helper can observe the behavior and suggest methods of improvement
7. Practicing the new behavior in the natural environment

Conclusions about Skills Training.   Although not all skills training programs include all of these components, most effective ones do. Many programs include other components as well. Sometimes the additional components are similar to cognitive restructuring or SD in that they are directed toward creating a better understanding of the communication process and eliminating fear and negative beliefs that might spawn negative self-statements.

Visualization

After many years of research and many publications, Hopf and Ayres (1992) have concluded that visualization is an appropriate treatment method for reducing communication apprehension and fear. Because we agree with their conclusion, we are including some of their work here.

The theoretical basis for visualization was first introduced by Assagioli (1973, 1976). More recently, Hopf and Ayres have used visualization to lessen communication apprehension and fear and improve communication performance in highly fearful individuals. *Visualization (VIS)* is "a procedure that encourages people to think positively about public speaking by taking them through a carefully crafted script" (see Ayres & Hopf, 1989, for a sample script) (Hopf and Ayres, 1992, p. 187).

You use visualization to picture the day of a presentation beginning full of energy and confidence and ending with a successful presentation. At the end of the visualization, you should congratulate yourself on a job well done. Throughout the process you are asked to practice relaxation and to think positively about each component of the process. You are to visualize your success. Visualization should be used to help high apprehensive, fear-filled people build their confidence about public presentations (for more detailed information, consult Hopf & Ayres, 1993).

SUMMARY

We have stressed that communication apprehension, communication avoidance, shyness, willingness to communicate, public speaking anxiety, and communication effectiveness are all interrelated. Communication apprehension/fear—whether generalized across communication contexts, specific to a given context, specific to a given receiver or group of receivers, or generated by a specific situation—is probably the single most important factor in causing ineffective communication.

A person who experiences communication apprehension (CA) is not the exception. Almost everyone experiences such apprehension or fear at one time or another: some more often than others. For those who experience it only rarely, it is not a major problem in our lives. For those who experience it to the point that it interferes with their daily lives or stands in the way of their personal or professional success, they need not accept this as something they have to endure.

As noted in this chapter, communication apprehension/fear can be substantially reduced by a variety of methods and has already been so reduced for literally thousands of individuals. Many schools and colleges have programs based on the methods discussed in this chapter available at little or no cost. In places where no such program is available, it is almost certain that a local clinical psychologist trained in the use of systematic desensitization and/or cognitive restructuring can provide the help needed. In addition, an increasing number of communication professors and specialists who can provide such help are making themselves available. The minimal cost of obtaining such help is far outweighed by the benefits obtained. If you feel you might benefit from such help, do not hesitate to seek it. Just like any other person with a problem (whether it be a fear of heights, spiders, flying, small spaces, large spaces, or relationships), seek help to reduce your fear of communication if you feel you need it and are willing to work with the professional helper.

CHAPTER

5   Your Image

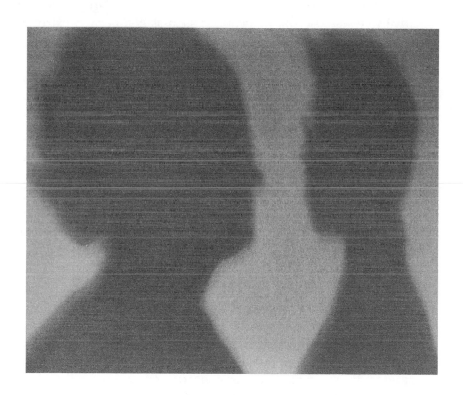

Although overcoming one's anxiety may be the most important first step for many speakers, the next step is critical in order to be effective. Part of the reason that we are concerned about anxiety is that we know receivers' perceptions of sources are critically important in the human communication process. This is because messages are interpreted through receivers' impressions of the source. How you are perceived by receivers will often have a major impact on whether receivers attend to, listen to, and believe what you are attempting to communicate. Five main categories of public perceptions can impact the receivers' perceptions of a presenter: Source credibility, source attractiveness, homophily/similarity, sociocommunicative style, and person perceptions such as composure, extroversion, and sociability. Each of these categories is reviewed in this chapter.

Perceptions of Your Image

How the audience views the speaker (or the source) may be divided into four types of perceptions. Source credibility is composed of competence, trustworthiness, and perceived caring (or goodwill). Source attractiveness is composed of physical attractiveness, social attractiveness, and task attractiveness. Source homophily (or similarity) is composed of attitude homophily and background homophily. In addition, the audience forms person perceptions of a speaker through source composure, extroversion, and sociability.

Source Credibility

The effects of source credibility have been studied more than any other public speaking variable. *Credibility* refers to how believable a source is seen to be. In other words, this is how believable your receivers(s) perceive you to be. McCroskey and Teven (1999) and others have determined three primary dimensions of source credibility that must be considered for listeners to perceive you as a highly credible source. These dimensions are competence, trustworthiness, and perceived caring or goodwill. An example of the current instrument used to measure these perceptions is presented in Table 5.1. (Tables 5.1 through 5.5 are provided so that you may analyze your image or the image of another speaker.) Although Tom Brokaw is given as an example, your instructor may ask you to evaluate the image of other speakers in your class as they

TABLE 5.1   Credibility Assessment Measure (CRED)

Directions: On the scales below, indicate your feelings about Tom Brokaw. Numbers 1 and 7 indicate a very strong feeling. Numbers 2 and 6 indicate a strong feeling. Numbers 3 and 5 indicate a fairly weak feeling. Number 4 indicates you are unsure or undecided.

Competence

Reliable	7	6	5	4	3	2	1	Unreliable
Uninformed	1	2	3	4	5	6	7	Informed
Unqualified	1	2	3	4	5	6	7	Qualified
Intelligent	7	6	5	4	3	2	1	Unintelligent
Valuable	7	6	5	4	3	2	1	Worthless
Inexpert	1	2	3	4	5	6	7	Expert

Caring

Cares about me	7	6	5	4	3	2	1	Does not care about me
Has my interests at heart	7	6	5	4	3	2	1	Does not have my interests at heart
Self-centered	1	2	3	4	5	6	7	Not self-centered
Concerned with me	7	6	5	4	3	2	1	Not concerned with me
Insensitive	1	2	3	4	5	6	7	Sensitive
Understanding	7	6	5	4	3	2	1	Not understanding

Trustworthiness

Honest	7	6	5	4	3	2	1	Dishonest
Untrustworthy	1	2	3	4	5	6	7	Trustworthy
Honorable	7	6	5	4	3	2	1	Dishonorable
Moral	7	6	5	4	3	2	1	Immoral
Unethical	1	2	3	4	5	6	7	Ethical
Phony	1	2	3	4	5	6	7	Genuine

Scoring

To compute your scores for competence, caring, and trustworthiness, simply add the numbers you circled for each measure separately.

Competence = _____   Caring = _____   Trustworthiness = _____

(continued)

TABLE 5.1   Continued

Step 1 is the score for Competence, Step 2 for Perceived Caring, and Step 3 for Trustworthiness.

Scores for each measure must be between 6 and 42.

Scores >35 = high competence, caring, or trustworthiness.

Scores between 30 and 35 = moderate competence, caring, or trustworthiness.

Below 30 causes a receiver to question a speaker's competence, perceived caring, or goodwill/trustworthiness.

Sources: J. C. McCroskey & V. P. Richmond (1996), *Fundamentals of human communication. An interpersonal perspective* (Prospect Heights, IL: Waveland Press); J. C. McCroskey (2001), *An introduction to rhetorical communication* (8th ed.) (Boston: Allyn and Bacon).

deliver their speeches. A careful analysis will help a speaker understand what element of his or her image needs improvement.

Competence.   This dimension of credibility refers to the degree to which you are perceived to be knowledgeable, competent, or expert in a given subject matter. Competence exists along a continuum ranging from completely incompetent to completely competent. The perception is also influenced by how competent receivers perceive themselves to be. On the one hand, on a scale of 6 to 42, if a receiver thinks a speaker's competence on the topic of safe sex is 38 and his or her own competence is 24, then the source is probably quite competent in the receiver's mind. On the other hand, if the receiver perceives her or his own competence to be 24 and that of the speaker to be 18, then in the receiver's mind, the speaker (you) is (are) probably not very competent. Higher competence equals higher perceptions of expertness and efficacy about a topic.

It is quite simple. Receivers' views of a speaker's competence have an impact on their overall response to that speaker. If receivers believe a speaker to be a competent and knowledgeable source, more competent than they are, then they are likely to embrace the speaker's opinions and follow his or her suggestions. If they perceive a speaker to be an incompetent and unknowledgeable source or, at least, less competent than they are, then the receivers are unlikely to embrace his or her opinions or follow the speaker's suggestions. Therefore, when attempting to be a competent public communicator, you must be perceived as competent. If you are not perceived to be competent, you may lose the audience at the beginning of the presentation. Once competence is lost, it may never be regained.

Trustworthiness. As receivers, we may feel that a presenter is competent on his or her topic. However, if we feel that we cannot trust the presenter to be honest with us, we are likely to think that person has little credibility. As with competence, trustworthiness must be high in the receivers' minds or a source might not be listened to, much less believed or trusted. For example, you may perceive a salesperson to be very knowledgeable (a 42 on our scale) with regard to a particular product. If you believe that salesperson to be dishonest and untrustworthy in dealing with you, the salesperson probably has low credibility in your mind.

As with competence, perceptions of trustworthiness exist along a continuum. Judgments of a source can range from being completely untrustworthy to completely trustworthy. This perception is *not* mediated by people's perceptions of their own trustworthiness. That is, how trustworthy or untrustworthy they believe themselves to be does not mediate how trustworthy they perceive another person to be. Higher trustworthiness equals higher perceptions of trust and honesty on a topic.

Perceived Caring or Goodwill. Receivers may feel that a presenter is both competent on his or her topic and trustworthy. However, if they feel that the presenter does not care about them or have their best interests at heart, they are likely to see that person as having little credibility. Perceived caring is the degree to which receivers perceive a source/speaker cares about their feelings, understands them, and has their concerns foremost in mind. As with competence and trustworthiness, perceptions of perceived caring exist along a continuum. Judgments of a source can range from being completely uncaring to completely caring. This perception is not mediated by receivers' perceptions of their own caring. That is, how caring or uncaring they believe themselves to be does not mediate how caring they perceive another person to be. Higher perceived caring equals higher perceptions of understanding and concern.

Credibility perceptions are one set of critical perspectives that influence receivers' responses to and attitudes about a presenter or speaker. Another important set of perceptions that relates to receivers' views is speaker attraction.

Source Attractiveness

When people think of interpersonal attraction, they usually think of the physical attributes of attraction. However, physical attractiveness is not the only form of attraction that affects people's reactions to a speaker or presenter. Like credibility, attraction has three dimensions. Besides their physical attractiveness, speakers are also judged on their social and task attractiveness. An instrument designed to measure each of these three dimensions is provided in Table 5.2. The measure is a combination of the McCroskey and McCain (1974) social and task measures of interpersonal attraction and a modified version of physical attraction.

Physical Attractiveness.   This dimension of *attractiveness* refers to the degree to which receivers perceive the source to be someone they are attracted to because of his or her physical and/or professional appearance. This physical attraction is based on what a person wears and/or how he or she looks. Although some would like to ignore this dimension of attraction, it is not possible. Whether or not you like it, this culture still places a high value on physical attractiveness. For example, many companies simply will not hire personnel who do not have the "look" that fits their organizations. For generations the culture of the United States has been a "looks-oriented" culture. In other words, to a major extent, it is not what you have to say that counts; it is how you look. Physical attractiveness carries its greatest impact in the first two minutes of a communication interaction. Within a few minutes receivers are making judgments about a source often based solely upon his or her physical appearance. To some extent, the perception of attractiveness can determine their affinity and willingness to listen to a source of information. Thus, it is important that you look like you want to give the speech; you should look like you have prepared your personal appearance for a speech in front of a number of people. You should be careful not to dress in such a way that your listeners are distracted by your clothing. However, you want to dress in such a way that the audience is impressed with your trustworthiness and competence. Although physical attraction is a critical variable in the communication process, it is not the only attractiveness variable by which we make judgments. We also judge others based on their perceived social and task attractiveness.

Social Attractiveness.   The dimension of social attractiveness refers to the degree to which receivers perceive a source to be someone with whom

TABLE 5.2   Assessment of Source Attraction

Directions: On the scales below, indicate how attractive you find Tom Brokaw to be. Numbers 1 and 7 indicate a very strong feeling. Numbers 2 and 6 indicate a strong feeling. Numbers 3 and 5 indicate a fairly weak feeling. Number 4 indicates you are unsure or undecided. SD=Strongly Disagree, SA=Strongly Agree.

Physical/Professional Appearance Attraction

1. I think he is quite professional in appearance.   SD 1 2 3 4 5 6 7 SA

2. He is very professional looking.   SD 1 2 3 4 5 6 7 SA

3. I find him very attractive professionally.   SD 1 2 3 4 5 6 7 SA

4. I don't like the way he looks.   SD 1 2 3 4 5 6 7 SA

Social Attraction

5. He could be a friend of mine.   SD 1 2 3 4 5 6 7 SA

6. It would be difficult to meet and talk with him.   SD 1 2 3 4 5 6 7 SA

7. He would not fit into my circle of friends.   SD 1 2 3 4 5 6 7 SA

8. We could never establish a friendship with each other.   SD 1 2 3 4 5 6 7 SA

Task/Job Attraction

9. He would be a typical goof-off when assigned a job to do.   SD 1 2 3 4 5 6 7 SA

10. I have confidence in his ability to get the job done.   SD 1 2 3 4 5 6 7 SA

11. When I want to get things done, I can usually depend on him.   SD 1 2 3 4 5 6 7 SA

12. I could not get anything accomplished with him.   SD 1 2 3 4 5 6 7 SA

Scoring

To compute your scores for the three dimensions of attraction, simply add the numbers you circled for each measure separately.

Physical = _____   Social = _____   Task = _____

Scores for each concept must be between 4 and 28.

Scores > 22 = higher physical, social, or task attraction.

they would like to spend time, have fun, and be entertained. Social attraction initially can be based on physical attraction, but after the first few minutes these two types of attraction may not be related. Initially social attraction is primarily based on how friendly, fun, and entertaining the source is perceived to be. Over time, no matter how physically attractive a source is, social attraction becomes a perception of how friendly or likable receivers consider the source to be.

For example, if you have ever been dissatisfied with a great-looking speaker, you have just separated physical attractiveness from social attractiveness. You might think the speaker is "easy on the eyes," but would be a boring, unfriendly, perhaps even a cold person with whom to associate. This type of speaker might be a knockout but also be about as entertaining as pond scum! By now you have stopped listening to the speaker and you are taking care of other tasks.

Social attractiveness of a source, then, is usually more important after the first few minutes. If receivers perceive a person to be attractive on a social level, they are likely to want future interactions with that person. Conversely, if they perceive the speaker to be lacking in social attractiveness, they are not likely to exert their communication energies with that particular source.

Task Attractiveness.   The third dimension of attractiveness refers to the degree to which receivers perceive the source as a desirable person with whom to establish a work or other task relationship. They see the source as task attractive when they view him or her as one with whom they would want to work, one who would be productive, one who is task-oriented, and one who is achievement-oriented. Task attraction is based on communication between speaker and receiver that is goal-oriented and effective for achievement of those goals.

Often when receivers perceive a source to be competent in a given task area, they will likely find that person to be an attractive one with whom to work in that area. An example of task attraction might be found in team groups. When preparing a report or task for a supervisor, your desire to work with a person will often be influenced in large part by how task- and work-oriented you perceive another team member to be. If you know that person is a solid task-oriented member of the team, then he or she will be more task attractive to you than will another team member who is great looking or a lot of fun but does poorly on task-oriented projects.

You should realize that each dimension of attractiveness is independent from the other dimensions. A source can be physically attractive but have little social or task attraction. A source can be socially attractive but have little physical or task attraction. A source can be task attractive but have little physical or social attraction. A source is attractive only to the degree you perceive him or her as attractive. When you perceive a source to be attractive, you are more likely to listen, learn, and retain information communicated by the source and be influenced by him or her.

Source Homophily or Similarity

Like credibility and attraction, homophily (the degree two persons are similar or are perceived by each other to be similar) has dimensions. People also judge speakers on their perceived attitude and background homophily. An instrument designed to measure each of these two dimensions of speaker homophily or similarity with the receiver is provided in Table 5.3. The measure was developed by McCroskey, Richmond, and Daly (1975).

Perceptions affecting our attitudes about and responses to a speaker are based on receivers' similarity to the speaker, technically known as *homophily*. The principle of homophily suggests that the more similar communicators are, the more likely they are to interact with one another, the more likely their communication will be successful. Simply put, the more similar speakers are to their receivers, the more communication there will be, and the more likely that communication will be successful. This is why some speakers are successful and others are not. For example, American women speaking on women's rights in the Islamic culture not only have low credibility and attractiveness to the male-dominated culture but also are perceived as completely, totally antithetical to the audience they are addressing. In fact, there might not even be an audience interested in hearing from these sources about this particular topic.

Attitude Homophily.   This type of homophily refers to the degree to which a receiver perceives her or his attitudes, beliefs, and values to be similar to those of the speaker. Again, this is a perception because one does not always know the attitudes of another person. As one gets to know another person, this attitude similarity perception is either reinforced or not reinforced by the communication between speaker and receiver. If a speaker seems similar to his or her audience because he or

TABLE 5.3   Assessment of Perceived Homophily/Similarity

Directions: On the scales below, indicate your feelings about Tom Brokaw. Numbers 1 and 7 indicate a very strong feeling. Numbers 2 and 6 indicate a strong feeling. Numbers 3 and 5 indicate a fairly weak feeling. Number 4 indicates you are unsure or undecided. There are no right or wrong answers.

Attitude Homophily

Tom Brokaw . . .

1. Is like me	7	6	5	4	3	2	1	Is unlike me
2. Is different from me	1	2	3	4	5	6	7	Is similar to me
3. Thinks like me	7	6	5	4	3	2	1	Does not think like me
4. Doesn't behave like me	1	2	3	4	5	6	7	Behaves like me

Background Homophily

Tom Brokaw . . .

1. Has status like mine	7	6	5	4	3	2	1	Has status different from mine
2. Is from social class different from mine	1	2	3	4	5	6	7	Is from social class similar to mine
3. Is culturally different	1	2	3	4	5	6	7	Is culturally similar
4. Has economic situation like mine	7	6	5	4	3	2	1	Has economic situation different from mine

Scoring

Add the numbers you circled for each measure separately.

Scores for each concept must be between 4 and 28.

Scores > 22 = higher attitudinal and background homophily/similarity.

Source: Reprinted by permission of Waveland Press, Inc. from J. C. McCroskey & V. P. Richmond, *Fundamentals of human communication: An interpersonal perspective* (Prospect Heights, IL: Waveland Press, Inc., 1996). All rights reserved.

she voices ideas and attitudes similar to the audience, then attitudinal homophily increases. If a speaker seems dissimilar to his or her audience because he or she voices ideas and attitudes dissimilar with the audience, then attitudinal homophily decreases. As perceived attitudinal homophily increases, so does receiver interest and willingness to be influenced by the speaker. As perceived attitudinal homophily decreases, so does receiver interest and willingness to be influenced by the speaker.

Charlton Heston voices similar attitudes and ideas about guns and gun control when addressing the National Rifle Association, whereas Sarah Brady does not voice similar attitudes and ideas about guns and gun control when addressing the National Rifle Association. Which would be seen as similar by NRA receivers?

Background Homophily.   Do Americans feel they have more in common with the Chinese? Or the British? Perhaps the answers would be as follows: No, Yes. Let us look at a few other examples. Would a person from Los Angeles feel he or she has more in common with a person from San Diego or one from Savannah, Georgia? Would a person from Birmingham, Alabama, feel he or she has more in common with a person from Atlanta or one from Fargo, North Dakota? These questions are concentrated on the idea of similarity in terms of background. The more similar two people are in terms of background, the more likely they are to communicate successfully. People from similar backgrounds often also have similar values, language, culture, preferred foods, and other orientations. People from dissimilar backgrounds are more likely to have dissimilar values, language, culture, foods, and orientations.

Background homophily is the similarity between persons based on shared background experiences, language, food, cultural norms, and so on. The greater the perceived similarity, the greater the likelihood for wanting to listen to and learn from the speaker. The greater the perceived similarity, the more frequent interactions between source and receiver. Therefore, because of these shared background experiences, the more effective the speaker will be. For example, Democratic Representative Sheila Jackson Lee would probably have more demographic similarity with the South or Southwest than would Senator Ted Kennedy.

It is essential that the speaker develop attitude and background homophily with his or her intended receivers. The more similar the speaker is with the audience, the more likely the presentation will be received well. Although the perceptions we have discussed all contribute to the receivers' perceptions of the speaker's image, three other perceptions still need to be reviewed. These people's perceptions are composure, extroversion, and sociability. The measure of these three perceptions is provided in Table 5.4.

TABLE 5.4   Composure, Extroversion, Sociability Assessment

Directions: On the scales below, indicate your feelings about Tom Brokaw. Circle the number between the adjectives that best represents your feelings about Tom Brokaw. Numbers 1 and 7 indicate a very strong feeling. Numbers 2 and 6 indicate a strong feeling. Numbers 3 and 5 indicate a fairly weak feeling. Number 4 indicates you are undecided or do not understand the adjectives themselves. There are no right or wrong answers. Work quickly and record your first response.

Composure

Nervous	1	2	3	4	5	(6)	7	Poised
Tense	1	2	3	4	5	(6)	7	Relaxed
Calm	7	6	(5)	4	3	2	1	Anxious
Excitable	1	2	3	4	(5)	6	7	Composed

Extroversion

Bold	7	6	5	(4)	3	2	1	Timid
Quiet	1	2	(3)	4	5	6	7	Verbal
Silent	1	2	3	(4)	5	6	7	Talkative
Aggressive	7	6	5	(4)	3	2	1	Meek

Sociability

Awful	1	2	3	4	5	6	(7)	Nice
Unpleasant	1	2	3	4	5	6	(7)	Pleasant
Irritable	1	2	3	4	5	6	(7)	Good Natured
Cheerful	(7)	6	5	4	3	2	1	Gloomy

Scoring

To compute your scores for the three perceptions, simply add the numbers you circled for each measure separately.

Composure = __22__   Extroversion = __15__   Sociability = __25__

To measure your perception of a different person, simply replace Tom Brokaw with the name.

Scores for each measure must be between 4 and 28.

The higher the score, the more composed, extroverted, and sociable you view Tom Brokaw.

Source: Reprinted by permission of Waveland Press, Inc. from J. C. McCroskey & V. P. Richmond, *Fundamentals of human communication: An interpersonal perspective* (Prospect Heights, IL: Waveland Press, Inc., 1996). All rights reserved.

Person Perception

Source Composure.   Perceptions of source composure refer to the emotional and physical control that the receiver perceives the speaker has. Composure is being viewed as in control, calm, cool, collected, comfortable with oneself, poised, and relaxed. The opposite of composure is being viewed as out of control, tense, uncomfortable, fidgety, nervous, apprehensive, and anxious. If a source is overly composed, then he or she might be viewed as cold, aloof, and distant. If a source is undercomposed, then he or she might be viewed as a nervous wreck. Therefore, the speaker walks a fine line between being comfortably composed and either under- or overcomposed. The better speakers seem relaxed, in control, calm, and comfortable while presenting information to an audience. Therefore, it is essential that speakers maintain their sanity and composure and put forth an image of a comfortable person talking with their audiences. Anything more and they might be perceived as too cold. Anything less and they might be perceived as not composed.

Extroversion.   The term *extroversion* refers to the degree to which a speaker is perceived by an audience as talkative, bold, outgoing, dynamic, active, and vibrant. The term *introversion* refers to the degree to which a speaker is viewed by an audience as withdrawn, quiet, detached, distant, and reserved. In the United States, people generally have a lower opinion of those who are introverted. In fact, those with introverted personalities are often judged as less talkative, less outgoing, less friendly, less socially attractive, less competent, and less likely to be a leader. Therefore, there is a clear benefit in appearing extroverted, but not overly so. When a speaker is overly extroverted, he or she is often viewed as aggressive, outspoken, dominating, domineering, pushy, and loud. As with composure, a moderate level of extroversion is needed without being overly extroverted or introverted. Either end of the continuum is a problem for the public presenter. Those who are overly extroverted may be perceived as too loud or overbearing. Those who are too introverted may be perceived as too quiet and withdrawn. When in doubt, it is still better in this culture to be overly extroverted than introverted. Extroverts do get listened to. Introverts do not. In fact, the introverted person's audience may be asleep!

Sociability.   Most people want to interact with and listen to people whom they perceive to be likable, friendly, pleasant, agreeable, and amiable. Perceptions of a speaker's sociability relate to how likable, pleasant, and amiable the speaker is assessed to be. Typically, if receivers perceive a speaker to be pleasant and likable, they are more likely to listen to and learn from this speaker. Typically, if they perceive a speaker to be harsh, rude, unlikable, unpleasant, and disagreeable, they are less likely to listen to and learn from this speaker. Sociability is often equated with friendliness. When friendliness is missing from the speaker's image, the speaker is viewed in a negative fashion. Therefore, speakers must strive to be seen as friendly and sociable by the audience in order to maintain a good speaker image.

Sociocommunicative Orientation

Assertiveness

Assertiveness is the capacity to make requests; actively disagree; express positive or negative rights and feelings; initiate, maintain, or disengage from conversations; and stand up for oneself without attacking another person. Terms commonly used to describe a person who engages in assertive communication behaviors are *willing to defend own beliefs, independent, forceful, strong personality, dominant, willing to take a stand and act as a leader,* and (of course) *assertiveness.*

Responsiveness

Responsiveness is the capacity to be sensitive to the communication of others, to be a good listener, to make others comfortable in communicating, and to recognize the needs and desires of others. Terms commonly used to describe a person who engages in responsive communication behaviors include *helpful, sympathetic, compassionate, sensitive to needs of others, sincere, gentle, warm, tender, friendly, understanding,* and (of course) *responsive to others.*

Table 5.5 is a sociocommunicative measure of assertiveness and responsiveness.

SUMMARY

There are, then, a number of factors present when a speaker begins to talk. These include credibility—the competence, trustworthiness, and goodwill that audience members feel are being expressed by the speaker.

TABLE 5.5   Sociocommunicative Orientation

Directions: This questionnaire lists twenty personality characteristics. Indicate in the space at the left of each item the degree to which you believe the characteristic applies to Tom Brokaw.

    5 = Strongly agree
    4 = Agree
    3 = Undecided or unsure
    2 = Disagree
    1 = Strongly Disagree

____x____ **1.** Helpful
____x____ **2.** Defends own beliefs
_____ **3.** Independent
____x____ **4.** Responsive to others
_____ **5.** Forceful
_____ **6.** Has a strong personality
____x____ **7.** Sympathetic
____x____ **8.** Compassionate
_____ **9.** Assertive
____x____ **10.** Sensitive to the needs of others
_____ **11.** Dominant
____x____ **12.** Sincere
____x____ **13.** Gentle
____x____ **14.** Willing to take a stand
____x____ **15.** Warm
____x____ **16.** Tender
____x____ **17.** Friendly
_____ **18.** Acts as a leader
_____ **19.** Aggressive
_____ **20.** Competitive

Scoring

Items 2, 3, 5, 6, 9, 11, 14, 18, 19, and 20 measure assertiveness.
Items 1, 4, 7, 8, 10, 12, 13, 15, 16, and 17 measure responsiveness.

(continued)

TABLE 5.5   Continued

Add your scores on these two sets of items to get your assertiveness and responsiveness scores.

Assertiveness scores > 58 = high assertiveness.

Assertiveness scores < 40 = low assertiveness.

Responsiveness scores > 64 = high responsiveness.

Responsiveness scores < 43 = low responsiveness.

Sources: V. P. Richmond & J. C. McCroskey (2001), *Organizational communication: Making work, work* (Boston: Allyn and Bacon); J. C. McCroskey & V. P. Richmond (1996), *Fundamentals of human communication: An interpersonal perspective* (Prospect Heights, IL: Waveland Press).

In addition, the audience is concerned about the physical, social, and task attraction of the speaker. Many of these judgments are being made on the basis of homophily or perceived similarity. To what extent do the audience members feel that the speaker is similar to each of them in attitude and background? Finally, an audience wants the speaker to feel composed, but not arrogant. As well the audience prefers a speaker who is somewhat extroverted and sociable. For many, these ideas may appear overly complex, but the important thing is for you as a speaker to present yourself as someone to whom the audience will like to listen.

EXERCISE

How can you increase your credibility, attractiveness, homophily, composure, extroversion, sociability, and sociocommunicative orientation? Give two ideas for each concept.

Credibility:
   Competence

   Trustworthiness

   Perceived caring or goodwill

Attractiveness:
  Physical

  Social

  Task

Homophily:
  Attitude

  Background

Other Person Perceptions:
  Composure

  Extroversion

  Sociability

Sociocommunicative Orientation:
  Assertiveness

  Responsiveness

6

Analyzing the Audience

The primary goal of a speech is to create a mutually satisfactory interaction between the speaker and the audience. Now that you have learned how to analyze the speaker, it is important to begin the process of analyzing the audience. This task is a much more complex one because there are several people in the audience, all of whom are in some way different. As you begin to analyze the audience of a speech class, you will notice that there are many similarities. Most of the people in the class are in the same general range of ages. Most are gathered for the purpose of getting a college degree. Many are from the same geographic area. Thus there is often a great deal of homophily among those in the audience.

Yet there are also differences. The majority of individual audience members will be different. Some are majoring in education, some in engineering, some in liberal arts, some in the fine arts, some in business. Even among those in business, a student may be majoring in accounting, economics, marketing, or management. The amount of time that one has been in school may vary. Some finish in four years or less, but most take longer. Some students begin school, stay out a while, and finish many years later. There are both males and females in the class. As we begin the process of analyzing the audience, we start with these demographic factors. However, we also discuss the attitudinal and goal factors that may be important for knowing your audience.

Demographic Factors

The demographic factors that may be important in analyzing the audience include age, gender, knowledge of the subject, occupation, economic status, religion, ethnic heritage, personal experience, and level of education. In most college speech classes not all apply and some are relatively easy to determine. Others call for making *inferences* about what you do not know, based on what you do know. One should be extremely careful, however, to avoid stereotyping while in the process of making these inferences.

Age

There are no rules about how old a person in class may be, but for the most part, we know that college students are going to be at least seventeen years old. This means that for some the first president of the United

States that they remember is Bill Clinton. If we look at students who are twenty-five years old, their first memories may be of Ronald Reagan. At age forty, one might remember Lyndon Johnson. It is doubtful, though, that a student in 2002 will remember when FDR was president or even Harry Truman. Analyzing the age of the audience in terms of the presidency is just one starting point. How many would recall when there were no CDs or no videotape recorders or no color television?

Each generation (about twenty years) has its own notions about what is important, about who is important, and even about how decisions are made. To understand all of these factors you need to know about how old the people in the audience are. Knowing the age alone is not the most significant factor, however. Assuming that you are going to speak on how mainstream media (newspapers and television) have become more like the tabloids, you need to use examples with which the audience members can identify. If the audience is composed of middle-age people, they may remember the Pentagon Papers or Watergate. Most younger people will not remember these events. Therefore, this younger audience can identify with examples about the coverage of Princess Diana's death or the sexual scandals of the Clinton administration.

Gender

Certainly attitudes and behavior about women have undergone a significant change over the past twenty-five to fifty years. People no longer automatically think of a man when they think of the police. No longer are all telephone repairpersons men. Although some people today maintain their perceptions of the traditional roles of women, many more contend that the roles in society are different today. Even so, it is likely that many men and women will have differing attitudes about certain topics. The topic of abortion, for example, carries with it substantial differences in thinking. The genders also differ in how they communicate, with most men maintaining a persuasive intent in most of their messages and most women desiring an attitude of negotiation and information (Tannen, 1994).

Take the topic of interior design. This topic can be used in a speech with which both males and females feel comfortable. It is known that women in general have a better concept of color than do men. Therefore, when talking about colors such as mauve, puce, indigo, and taupe, the effective speaker might want to *show* the colors to demonstrate how they differ from purple, red, blue, and beige.

Knowledge of the Subject

Once a football player began his speech on football to a class at a school in the Southeastern Conference. He began his speech with "This is a football." Everyone in the class knew what a football was. Class members felt he was talking down to them. If he had begun by saying that many fans know the basics of the game but that he would explain some of the intricacies, then they probably would have listened to the rest of his speech. It is important that a speaker neither overestimate the knowledge of listeners (for example, speaking about the details of creating one's own Web site on a computer) or underestimate them (as did the football player). In a speech class, the speaker can assume that the members of the audience have had certain experiences, that they have a certain level of intelligence, and that they can listen better when the speech is directed to their level of knowledge.

Occupation

Occupation is one of those factors that often does not apply in the speech classroom. However, in today's world, many students do work part-time or full-time. A speech on customer service will have an impact on all of the students as they are all customers, but some members of the class may be waiters, waitresses, or retail salespersons. They may look at your speech differently from those who do not have such jobs.

Probably more important for the classroom, though, is the *major* that a student in the audience in the class may have. For example, if most of the students are majoring in the fine arts, they might be less likely to understand principles of physics that relate to the acoustics of a stereo system. If most of the students in the class are majoring in accounting, they may have a better idea of how the stock market works and how to interpret daily reports on the Dow Jones Industrial Average and NASDAQ. Art majors may have more knowledge about Photo Shop and Quark Express computer programs, whereas accounting majors may better understand Excel and Quicken.

Most classes will have a variety of majors represented in them. The effective speaker must find a position in between simple and complex so that all of the students get something out of the speech but also so that no one is bored. The level of the student may also be important here. If the audience members are mostly freshmen, then the speaker can rest assured that most of them have not yet taken courses in the complex areas of their majors.

The effective speaker should also think about the past and future of her audience members. All of the students would have attended high school, and most would have done so in the United States. Therefore, a speech on how we can improve kindergarten through the twelfth grade might be a topic with which all of the students can identify. In addition, all of the students will have a future occupation, a job, a family, friends, personal problems, and so forth. Thus, topics such as how to buy life insurance, how to buy your first home, the high costs of funerals, taking care of the elderly, raising children, and interviewing for a job are ones that most will encounter regardless of their current major.

Once you give a speech elsewhere, it is important to determine what kinds of jobs the people in the audience might have. Where do they work? Do they get paid by the hour or are they on salary? What are their working conditions? Do they have families? Are they professionals? Why have they gathered together for this speech? A civic group, for example, such as Kiwanis, Lions, Civitans, Optimists, and the like, is generally composed of the people who run the town. Most are professionals. But you may be asked to speak to a study club, a garden club, a professional association, or a church group. The essential question to ask yourself is what is the commonality of the people in the audience so that you can speak to that commonality and find ways in which you and they have homophily.

Economic Status

For virtually all people, money is an important part of their lives. For an audience member who has difficulty making it from paycheck to paycheck or from semester to semester, there is probably little thrill in hearing a speaker discuss diversifying his or her stock portfolio. Fortunately for students in college, many find themselves in the same boat. Thus, analyzing the economic standing of people in the audience may not appear to be difficult, at least not at first. However, there are single parents who are working and attending college at the same time. Other students have parents who pay for their entire college expenses. So, although there is not as much diversity in a speech class as there might be later in life, a speaker needs to be concerned about this factor. As well, the topics that might be associated with money may be of interest to almost anyone. For example, using coupons to save at grocery stores, ordering textbooks over the Internet, shopping at discount stores: these are topics about which almost any audience would like to hear.

Religion

Depending on where in the country you are located, you can probably define the majority religion of the people in your audience. Certainly there are pockets in the United States in which Catholicism is the dominant religion; in others Protestant denominations (sometimes specific ones) are dominant. You should, nevertheless, realize that not everyone in a class or an audience is of the dominant religion. At most colleges there are Hindus, Moslems, atheists, agnostics, Baptists, Methodists, Mormons, Catholics, and Jewish people. It is important to recognize that within a particular religion views may be different. The religion is only one way in which they differ. Some religions are tied to ethnic and geographical regions; others are not. Some have stated views on such practices as drinking alcoholic beverages and abortion that may differ from their counterparts. An effective speaker should take special care not to offend his or her audience members because of their religions.

Ethnic Heritage

Another difference among audience members is their ethnic heritage. This means that they differ in ancestry, race, or religion. Although some black Americans share a common African American heritage, those of Asian descent share a different heritage. Some people from South America, Cuba, Puerto Rico, and Mexico may share a common Hispanic tradition. White Americans may share a European American heritage. Each group may differ in religion, food they like to eat, food they do not like to eat, music they like to listen to, and language. In today's world, we have diversity in most colleges. Therefore, we need to have a healthy respect for this diversity. Again, the speaker who focuses on commonalities instead of differences will most likely be more effective.

Personal Experience

Although all of the other factors we have mentioned tell us something about audience members, we should also remember that *individual* experiences have a major impact on audience members. Although one's religion may not be the major factor, a student who has had an abortion may feel quite differently about a speech on abortion than do other class members who have never encountered the situation personally. The same may be true if an audience member has had a relative die of AIDS or some other disease such as lung cancer. Obviously a speaker cannot know the personal experiences of all of the members of the audience, but the speaker should be careful to avoid offending or hurting people in the audience who may have had experiences that affect how a speech will influence them.

Level of Education

In a speech class, the level of education for almost everyone is about the same. All of the students have graduated from high school or received a GED. In most institutions, the students have taken the same courses through the first year and into the second year. The students in class should certainly know some basic mathematics as well as English, basic social studies (including history), and basic elements of science. Educated people know how to recognize correct grammar, with which the speaker should be concerned. Educated people know the differences between "high" culture and "pop" culture. Many educated people would have visited other parts of the country and other parts of the world.

From all of this, then, you can establish some general guidelines about what you know about the audience (in the classroom). Without much help, you can make preliminary assessments about age and gender, you know something about the level of education, you may be able to assess economic status in that the same students do not attend two-year colleges and Ivy League institutions. When audience members are introduced in class, you learn something about whether and where they work. You may also learn about whether they are married, are divorced, have children, went to high school with another member of the class, and so forth. You might discover something about their religion; if not, you may learn about it when they speak. It is important to remember that people make judgments after they discover information. These judgments are inferences, but people need to be careful that their inferences do not turn into stereotypes. Not every southerner is a goober. Not every New Yorker is assertive. Each individual has personality characteristics. And most of them will be quite open to what you have to say because they will want you to listen to them. As we expand, ever so slightly, this notion of audience analysis, however, we discuss philosophical orientation.

Philosophical Orientation

Unfortunately, you cannot always discover one's philosophical orientation. Even if you asked someone to tell you his or her philosophical orientation, you may not get a good answer. In fact, you may not get an answer at all. In the next few paragraphs, we describe a few of these orientations to help guide you about how people think.

An *empirical orientation* is the viewpoint of one who believes that the only types of information that should be and can be discussed are those that can be observed scientifically. Many engineers and scientists take this position. It involves a strict organizational pattern in which matters are handled step by step. This is certainly the view of mathematics: Each math course requires a prerequisite; by skipping courses, you simply make your life difficult. Some people, however, take this a little too far. For example, a couple (both engineers) contrived a series of hundreds of rules for each other to obey once they got married: No clothes on the floor, or there was a penalty. No staying up past midnight, or a penalty would ensue. Empirically oriented persons often have trouble understanding art, which appears to lack the kind of certainty that empiricists want in their lives.

A *libertarian orientation* is a philosophical perspective in which individuals think that individual rights go beyond the government. Such persons would probably be in favor of legalizing marijuana—in fact, in favor of legalizing all drugs. They might also favor no speed limits on highways, no government interference in the business world, less taxes, less government, fewer government workers. The idea is that people should be responsible for their own lives.

Pragmatically oriented individuals are concerned primarily that things work. They are interested in the most effective manner of doing things. They might prefer speeches that explain how to finish college more quickly, how to be ensured that they will get a job after college, how to balance their checkbooks adequately. These people may purchase practical gifts for their loved ones on their anniversaries. They might disagree with a libertarian about the speed limits or the legalization of drugs because they feel that the proposals would not work.

One with an *existential orientation* might believe that people's lives are in the here and now. They should pay less attention to problems that may occur in the future because the problems may never occur. The existential person is interested in experiencing life; thus, whereas the pragmatic person may not like to hear a speech about bungee jumping or skydiving, the existential person may love those topics. You should not get the impression, though, that an existential person is necessarily hedonistic ("life is about pleasure"). An existentialist may be quite serious about the freedom that he or she possesses as a result of being a decision-making individual.

The *aesthetic person* may be more interested in those aspects of life that lack black-and-white answers (unlike the empirical person). Aesthetes may be interested in determining what are good and bad films or artwork. Their thinking is more creative than it is practical or empirical. They may be more concerned about how the speech sounds than what it says.

There are many other aspects that could be discussed and that might be helpful including conservative versus liberal approaches to life and government. In addition, some think in terms of time. Some people are more past-oriented; others future, still others present. Nevertheless, you need to learn and *remember* as much as you can about individual audience members to help assess what they might want to hear or how you can state your case so that they will be more receptive to it (see Table 6.1).

SUMMARY

Audience analysis is an extremely important aspect of presenting a speech. Using demographic data such as age, gender, knowledge of the subject, occupation, economic status, religion, ethnic heritage, personal experience, and level of education, you have the basic information to infer additional qualities such as philosophical perspective. Speaking to a group of Internal Revenue Service (IRS) agents about nonverbal communication, one might choose to talk about how to detect deception. Certainly the IRS agents would like to have information about how to tell whether a person is lying (pragmatic orientation). Speaking to engineers, one would know that the speech should be structured well, step-by-step. Artists, however, would prefer looking at criteria that are aesthetic in nature. In considering all of these factors, there is little wonder that some people say that majors choose their students instead of students choosing their majors.

TABLE 6.1   Audience Analysis Form

Directions: Complete this form about what you think you know about your class after the first day or two. Then, go back and check your views toward the end of the class.

_____ 1. Number of people in class who are seventeen to twenty years old

_____ 2. Number of people in class who are twenty-one to forty years old

_____ 3. Number of men and of women in the class

_____ 4. Number of students who work part time or full time

_____ 5. Number of students who have been skydiving

_____ 6. Number of students who regularly attend religious service

_____ 7. Number of students who own a computer

_____ 8. Number of students who live on campus

_____ 9. Number of students who own their home

_____ 10. Number of students in class who are divorced

_____ 11. Number of students in class who have children

_____ 12. Number of students in class who smoke cigarettes

_____ 13. Number of students from outside the United States

_____ 14. Number of Protestant students in the class

_____ 15. Number of students who took a vocational course in high school

_____ 16. Number of students who will withdraw from this course before it is over

As a result of these numbers, how do you feel your audience is likely to consider a speech you would give?

CHAPTER

7 Listening

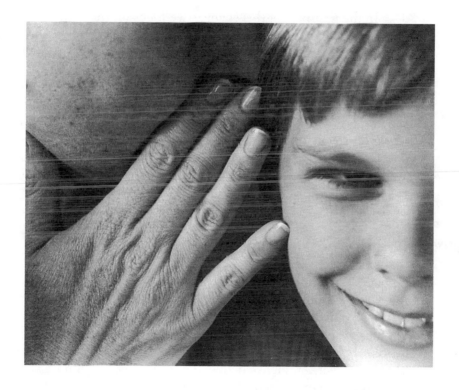

As people attempt to monitor their own images and to analyze audiences, they find they need to monitor the talking and thinking of themselves and others. The basic process they use to monitor is listening. *Listening* may be defined as the "conscious, cognitive effort involving primarily the sense of hearing (reinforced by other senses) and leading to interpretation and understanding" (Nathan, 1964, p. 24). In a public speaking situation, there are various aspects of the listening process. The audience members need to listen carefully so that they may gain from the speech. The speaker must make a special effort to encourage the audience to listen.

In the first part of this chapter, we focus on the responsibility of the speaker. Getting people to listen, comprehend, and understand a message is challenging under the most favorable of conditions. Even when one is motivated to listen, circumstances and internal or external noise may interfere with the communication process. This segment reviews the five selectivity processes that can directly interfere with reception, listening, and comprehension of messages during the speaking process. These five types of selectivity processes are selective exposure, selective attention, selective perception, selective retention, and selective recall. As speakers we must recognize each selectivity process and how each one can become an obstacle to effective information and communication processing.

Selectivity and the Speaking Process

Human communication is an ongoing, ever-changing, nonstatic process. Many times a person will select to listen or not to listen to the other person or persons involved in this process. This capacity to select when to listen, thus absorbing information, is often overlooked as a significant part of the process. If, however, individuals can become more aware of the tendency to listen selectively or not listen, then the communication process can be more effective. People who actively listen to messages from others are generally perceived as more responsive, competent communicators. People who do not listen to messages from others are generally perceived as unresponsive, incompetent communicators. In addition, people who do not listen and attend to messages from others are often perceived as cold, aloof, rude, and uncaring communicators. By electing not to listen, individuals also receive less information to use when making decisions, responding to other people, and establishing and maintaining relationships.

Selective Exposure

Selective exposure refers to a listener's conscious or unconscious choice to receive messages from a specific source. Most people engage in this type of behavior on a daily basis. People, consciously or unconsciously, decide which television shows to watch, with whom to communicate, to whom to listen, and whom to "tune out." Often these decisions are based on preference for the subject or person. Receivers make predictions about the nature of the message through their knowledge of the speaker. Students who have negative affect for an instructor do not listen to the instructor. Therefore, they may perform less well in the class than do students who have positive affect for the same instructor. Employees who have negative affect for a supervisor do not listen well to the supervisor. Therefore, they may perform less well in the work environment. To overcome this first obstacle to speaking effectiveness, then, we need to understand the five factors that lead to selective exposure.

Utility. Content that seems useful or interesting is more likely to be selected for exposure than content that seems less useful. For example, people who want to learn more about home improvement might select to listen to Bob Vila. Students who want to know the top ten videos of the week often tune in to VH1 or MTV.

Enlightened Self-Interest. Beneficial or advantageous information often receives more exposure from people. For example, many infomercials work on this factor. An infomercial related to making more money receives a large amount of exposure from the public because most persons can see immediate benefits. Therefore, if managers want employees to expose themselves to information presented in meetings, managers need to be able to answer the question "What will this do for me?" If this question cannot be answered, then many employees simply will not expose themselves to the managers' information.

Proximity. Information that is immediately available or close to a person is most likely to be selected for exposure. Consequently, if a speaker wants to persuade a receiver, then the source must be available for communication when the receiver wants to communicate. Marketing experts recognize when to offer certain advertisements and how to make the ad seem "proximately close" to the audience. For example, many food chains and restaurants put commercials on during the prime time preceding the evening meal. If the food chain or restaurant being advertised is in a person's kitchen (so to speak), then the person feels closer to the restaurant. Consequently, the now hungry person is more likely to get in a car and go directly to the restaurant advertised.

Involvement.   The more important a topic is to a person, the more exposure the person will seek. For example, most avid football fans never miss the Super Bowl. These fans seek more information, become more involved with the sport, videotape the game, and rarely listen to anything negative about the sport. Sports fans want to talk about football and other sports. Therefore, if the question "How can this person be involved in this topic?" cannot be answered, then the person to whom the topic is directed might not listen. Often people ask, "Why should I listen to this?" Or "How does this topic relate to me?"

Consistency and Reinforcement.   People allow for exposure to information that is both consistent with and reinforcing of their viewpoints. It is usual for people simply to tune out the information or the source sending information that is inconsistent with and not reinforcing of the person's attitudes, beliefs, and values.

Selective Attention

Selective attention occurs when a listener cannot control the types of messages to which he or she is exposed. Thus, because the listener cannot avoid exposure to the message, the listener simply selects not to pay attention to the message, but to pay attention to something else. Occasionally in church, young and older people alike cannot avoid exposure to the sermon, but they can select not to pay attention to the sermon, instead choosing to write notes, whisper, count the number of people in church, or gaze out a window. This type of selective attention behavior occurs in many facets of life such as business meetings, speeches, lectures, and so on. As with selective exposure, many factors contribute to determining which messages are given attention at any given time. The five factors that influence selective attention follow.

Attention Span.   No matter what people choose to pay attention to, that attention can last only so long. Children have shorter attention spans than adults. For example, many children can pay attention to a speaker for only a few seconds or what is known as "commercial time." Adults can usually pay attention to a source for about fifteen to twenty minutes before their attention span wanes. Television programmers are very aware of this attention span factor. This explains why shows such as *Sesame Street, Mr. Rogers' Neighborhood,* and *Barney* are such big hits with children: These shows are filled with brief, attention-getting messages that are adapted for children. Television shows such as *60 Minutes, Dateline,* and *20/20* are designed in segments of fifteen to twenty minutes for the adult population. Thus, if a speaker wants a listener to stay attentive, then he or she should design the message so it is compatible with the receiver's attention span. A speaker should always ask him or herself, "Is this message too long? Should I condense the message? Who is the intended receiver of this message?"

Novelty.   Speakers, messages, and things that are unusual, different, or distinctive can maintain listeners' attention longer than the ordinary, usual, or commonplace things. When traveling, Texans may pay little attention to cows. However, New Yorkers (those from the city) might give more attention to cows because they do not usually see many. VH1 has been very successful with its Pop Up Video format, which is different, distinctive, unusual, and novel. People are attracted to the idiosyncratic, fascinating formatting of this particular segment of VH1. Additionally, Pop Up Video segments are "short enough" so a person's attention span does not deteriorate. A source should ask, "Is this message novel or different? Will this message catch another person's attention?"

Concreteness.   Messages that are simple, clear, concrete, easy to understand, straightforward, tangible, and interesting are easier to pay attention to than are messages that are abstract, intangible, confusing, or obscure. Most listeners do not like to search for meaning behind a message or from a speaker. Consequently, we need to transmit messages that are real, easy to understand, and clear. In addition, messages should relate to what listeners understand and/or have experienced. The rule is KISS or "keep it short and sweet" or as some put it "keep it simple, stupid." Speakers who send messages that are too complex, abstract, and boring will not hold the attention of receivers for very long.

Size.   In general, bigger things tend to draw more attention than small things. If a speaker really wants receivers to hear or read a message, then the message should be set apart, enlarged, or emphasized. Billboards along highways are often very simple, yet functional, ways of catching people's attention. They are large and attract attention because of their size and novelty.

Length. Attention is often directed toward messages that are <u>moderate</u> in <u>length</u> (written) or <u>duration</u> (time). Very brief messages may be ignored or missed. Very lengthy messages may be ignored because they are too long, are confusing, or may be misinterpreted because too many ideas are included. If a speaker must communicate a large amount of information, it is desirable to do so with messages that are devoted to smaller chunks of information. Therefore, the speaker should <u>organize</u> and <u>chunk, explain, or delete information before delivery.</u> A good assumption to follow is if the message can be communicated in more concise terms, then do so.

Selective Perception

Messages do not carry meanings. The meanings behind the messages are in the minds of the listeners. *Selective perception* is the process of attributing <u>meaning to messages.</u> The meaning that is stimulated by a speaker depends on both the message and the receiver. Several factors will be considered that may cause a receiver to select perceptions different from those intended by the source.

Puzzling Messages. Messages are often ambiguous, uncertain, imprecise, and open to misinterpretation and misunderstanding. Words that a speaker uses in different ways can lead a listener, even a listener who is trying diligently to get the speaker's intended meaning, to choose a meaning other than the meaning the speaker intended. Often this confusion can be managed by encouraging people to <u>ask clarifying questions</u>, by <u>not using too many complex words</u>, and by <u>not using abstract terms</u> or language above the receiver's level of knowledge.

Absence of Message Redundancy. Message redundancy enables the listeners to have a second or third opportunity to comprehend the intended meaning behind a speaker's message. <u>Single messages</u> are far <u>more likely to be misunderstood</u> than are multiple messages addressed toward stimulating the equivalent meaning in the mind of the receiver. The rule is to say it once, say it twice, say it three times, and hope the receivers will get the intended meaning. It should be noted that whereas an English teacher may argue against redundancy, a speech teacher may be in favor of it. The reason is that one can go back and look at a written message, but if the listener misses a point the first time, it needs to be repeated.

Absence of a Listener Schema. Receivers learn by assigning information into categories. Category systems of this nature are known as *schema*. A speaker must help his or her listeners create a schema for new ideas. This means the speaker must keep talking and using a variety of words and language until the lightbulb turns on in the listener's mind.

Early Experiences. Most speakers and listeners know the world through their past or early experiences. The experiences of a person growing up in the 1980s are different from those of a person growing up in the 1990s. The 1980s person has a breadth of experiences that may be very dissimilar to those of the 1990s person. Therefore, both speakers and receivers need to try to understand and relate to the experiences and backgrounds of one another. This means constantly learning and relearning concepts, language, and meaning.

Assumptions and Biases. An *assumption* is a guess, conjecture, or hypothesis about how another person will react or communicate. A *bias* is a preconception, opinion, or evaluation of another person. Essentially all people have assumptions and biases about other people. Whenever the listener has assumptions or biases related to a speaker's message, it is possible that the message will be perceived in a way that is consistent with the speaker's intent. Unfortunately, this is more the exception than the norm. People tend to perceive what they expect to see or hear and are most likely to interpret messages in such a manner that the message conforms to their *own* assumptions and biases. Selective perception will always occur to some extent, but if a speaker seeks feedback from the receivers, then communication may be more effective and perception may become more accurate.

Selective Retention

Selective retention is the decision of whether to save information in long-term memory. Often the barriers of selective exposure, attention, and perception are overcome, but listeners' retention is only short term. Some people refer to this short-term retention as "in one ear and out the other ear." Consequently, speakers must work to encourage listeners to store information in long-term memory so the information can be recalled when needed. This is very similar to most word processing packages. A user often cannot exit a document without the system asking, "Do you want to save document?" Generally, the answer is "yes." Then the document is saved so it can be recalled or retrieved at a later date. Unfortunately, listeners' brains don't have this feature. Several factors are known to influence selective retention.

Absence of Highlighting.   This lack of highlighting can result in the information being lost. Often students do not know what teachers expect, so they attempt to store too much information or give up and forget all of the information. Educators are often very good at highlighting relevant information. Highlighting can be accomplished by giving out learning objectives, speaking articulately, giving notes, writing on the chalkboard, giving significant points and terms to know, and reemphasizing significant content points for each unit.

Absence of Redundancy.   This lack of redundancy does not give the opportunity for a variety of ways in which to learn and retain material. Redundancy assumes that the more a listener hears or sees information, the more likely he or she is to recall the information. For children it is extremely critical that redundancy is used on a regular basis. Redundancy may not always be needed for adults. However, when in doubt about whether a person understands a message the way in which it was intended, say it again, using different terms, different examples. In other words, review the ideas in a variety of ways until the receiver understands the concept.

Absence of a Schema.   Listeners often do not save or store information because of a lack of schema. When listeners do not have a schema, or mental filing system, for information, it often filters out. Therefore, speakers need to help construct a schema or filing system for new information so that our listeners can save and retrieve the information.

Absence of Tangible Application.   In order for listeners to store and then recall or retrieve information, the information must have real, concrete applications. For example, when a physics teacher suggests, "This model will be used later in life," students often do not store the nebulous idea. Generally, listeners need "handles" or clear practical application of information before it is saved for retrieval.

Primacy and Recency Principles.   Generally, information reviewed first in a message (primacy principle) and information reviewed last (recency principle) are the most recalled items of information. Therefore, when presenting information, remember that ideas presented near the beginning or the conclusion of the message are likely to be easier for listeners to retrieve. Additionally, this information may be more effective than information presented in the middle of a presentation because of the primacy–recency principles. Speakers, businesspersons, and teachers who use the primacy–recency principles usually have receivers who perform better in recalling information.

Selective Recall

Selective recall is the successful retrieval of information. A speaker must attempt to affirm, through effective communication and overcoming the obstacles associated with selectivity, that a listener can recall messages sent by the speaker. If a listener never had selective exposure to information, then the information cannot be recalled. If a listener paid little attention to the information, then the information may not be recalled or may be recalled incorrectly. If the listener had a different perception about the information than did the speaker, then perception may be distorted. If a listener did not have or could not create a schema for incoming information, then the information may be lost. If a listener had little or no retention of information, then recall of the information is almost impossible. For example, in grade school through high school, students get a break from school in the summer months. During this break time, the students are often not retaining much of the information from the school year. Therefore, in the fall, when the school year begins, many teachers spend the first few weeks exposing students to content they had in the past but have lost over the summer. When there is a significant time span between selective exposure, attention, perception, and retention, then selective recall is limited.

Effective speaking is not an effortless task. The degree to which a listener chooses to expose him or herself to, chooses to attend to, perceives, stores, and recalls a message from a speaker is often associated with effective communication and comprehension. If speakers strive to eliminate the significant selectivity barriers, then the speaking process can be more successful.

Monitoring the Audience

The speaker must be able to monitor an audience while he or she is speaking. As mentioned in the beginning of this chapter, listening primarily involves the auditory sense (hearing), but it also involves the other senses, especially the visual sense when the speaker is speaking. The speaker must have eye contact with people in the audience to determine whether they are going asleep, are carefully listening, or appear confused. Monitoring the nonverbal behavior of audience members is critical so that the speaker can adapt the message. If the speech appears to be going all right until a certain point is reached and the listeners then appear confused, the speaker can say, "Should I repeat that?" When the audience members nod their heads, the speaker knows that some adaptation is needed and he or she can repeat using other words.

The speaker should "listen" for all types of nonverbal cues including nodding of heads in agreement, shaking of heads in disagreement, wide-eyed looks of amazement, smiling enthusiasm, and looks of puzzlement. The effective speaker is a good monitor. The speaker may even ask an audience member a question about a response during the speech or later. Nonverbal aspects of public speaking will be discussed in more detail in the next chapter.

Audience Responsibility

The primary responsibility of audience members is to try to avoid typical "traps" of listeners. The fact of the matter is that people spend so much time listening that they often forget that it takes a great deal of effort to be good at it. Listening is an active process, not a passive process. The good listener listens to a speech as if he or she will be tested on it later (see Tables 7.1, 7.2, and 7.3). In so doing, there is a focus not only on the facts and details of the speech but also on the primary purpose of the speech and its

TABLE 7.1   Listening Notes for an Informative Speech

This page can be used as a method to encourage more careful listening when a speaker is trying to inform the audience.

Name of Speaker _____

Topic _____

What are the major points of the speech?

What are some unusual facts in the speech?

What is the general purpose of the speech?

What questions do I have for the speaker?

central idea. The effective listener must also be open to the ideas of the speaker, not constantly in the process of thinking of ways to argue after the speech is completed. The effective listener can also disregard negative aspects of nonverbal and verbal communication on the part of the speaker so that he or she can pay more attention to the significant positive aspects.

Listeners should not interrupt a speaker unless the speaker has told them that they may do so. Listeners should wait to enter a room in which someone is speaking until the speech is over, or until there is a break for questions. Listeners also should not leave the room until the speech is concluded or until there is a break for questions. In order to remember questions for the speaker, a listener should write them down.

TABLE 7.2 Listening Notes for a Persuasive Speech

This page can be used to create better listening habits when a speaker delivers a persuasive speech.

What are the main points?

Do I agree or disagree? Why?

What new facts am I hearing?

What is the general purpose of the speech?

What questions do I have for the speaker?

As members of the audience, several practical guides may help listeners:

- Try to eliminate all distractions. Focus your attention only on the speaker and what the speaker has to say.
- Pretend that you are going to have a test on the material the speaker is covering. If the speech is about your benefits with the company, the speech will likely contain information that is important to your retirement.
- Find practical reasons for listening to the speech.
- Listen to see how the speech is organized. If the speaker says there are four reasons for doing something, try to remember what the four reasons are.

TABLE 7.3   Willingness to Listen Measure

Directions: The following twenty-four statments refer to the willingness to listen. Indicate in the space at the left of each item the degree to which the statement applies to you.

1 = Strongly Agree
2 = Agree
3 = Undecided
4 = Disagree
5 = Strongly Disagree

_____   1. I dislike listening to boring speakers.

_____   2. Generally, I can listen to a boring speaker.

_____   3. I am bored and tired while listening to a boring speaker.

_____   4. I will listen when the content of a speech is boring.

_____   5. Listening to boring speakers about boring content makes me tired, sleepy, and bored.

_____   6. I am willing to listen to boring speakers about boring content.

_____   7. Generally, I am unwilling to listen when there is noise during a speaker's presentation.

_____   8. Usually I am willing to listen when there is noise during a speaker's presentation.

_____   9. I am accepting and willing to listen to speakers who do not adapt to me.

_____   10. I am unwilling to listen to speakers who do not do some adaptation to me.

_____   11. Being preoccupied with other things makes me less willing to listen to a speaker.

_____   12. I am willing to listen to a speaker even if I have other things on my mind.

_____   13. While being occupied with other things on my mind, I am unwilling to listen to a speaker.

_____   14. I have a willingness to listen to a speaker, even if other important things are on my mind.

_____   15. Generally, I will not listen to a speaker who is disorganized.

_____   16. Generally, I will try to listen to a speaker who is disorganized.

(continued)

TABLE 7.3   Continued

_____ **17.** While listening to a nonimmediate, nonresponsive speaker, I feel relaxed with the speaker.

_____ **18.** While listening to a nonimmediate, nonresponsive speaker, I feel distant and cold toward that speaker.

_____ **19.** I can listen to a nonimmediate, nonresponsive speaker.

_____ **20.** I am unwilling to listen to a nonimmediate, nonresponsive speaker.

_____ **21.** I am willing to listen to a speaker with views different from mine.

_____ **22.** I am unwilling to listen to a speaker with views different from mine.

_____ **23.** I am willing to listen to a speaker who is not clear about what he or she wants to say.

_____ **24.** I am unwilling to listen to a speaker who is not clear, not credible, and abstract.

Scoring
Your score can range from 24 to 120.
Step 1: Add scores for items 2, 4, 6, 8, 9, 12, 14, 16, 17, 19, 21, and 23.
Step 2: Add scores for items 1, 3, 5, 7, 10, 11, 13, 15, 18, 20, 22, and 24.
Step 3: WLM = 64 − Total from Step 1 + Total from Step 2.

Scores above 80 indicate a high willingness to listen.

Scores below 50 indicate a low willingness to listen.

- Listen to see if you can determine the central idea of the speech. What is the specific purpose the speaker is trying to accomplish?
- As a critical listener, determine the sources of the speaker's information. Are the sources biased? If so, in what direction? How old is the information? Are there other sources that you know that might disagree?
- Does the logic of the speaker make sense? For example, if President George W. Bush says that we need to have a massive tax cut, based on projected surpluses, what if there are fewer surpluses because of the tax cuts?
- What are the responses of the other people in the audience? Are they bored, disagreeing, agreeing, concerned, frustrated?

- If you were going to give a speech in support of this one, what would you add?
- If you were going to give a speech opposing this one, what might you say?
- Remember, at all times, to listen to all that the speaker says—so that you understand before you begin analyzing.

SUMMARY

Listening involves the selectivity of information in a speech, being careful to expose oneself to all aspects of what the speaker is saying. Speakers must ensure that the audience members are listening by using such elements as utility, proximity, and involvement. Because listeners are selective, the speaker needs to emphasize important points, repeat them, and make them concrete. The speaker needs to be clear, monitoring the audience for instances of puzzlement and rephrasing the point when necessary. Speakers must highlight important points for the listeners, be redundant, illustrate a schema, and establish applications of the thoughts they are transmitting.

Constant monitoring on the part of listeners and speakers makes for an effective speaking situation. Both verbal and nonverbal aspects of a speech are part of the monitoring process. Listeners should be open to the speaker's ideas, listening as if there will be a test. Finally, listeners should be courteous to the speaker.

EXERCISES

1. In groups, students should discuss teacher or class variables that may cause students to give more attention during class (e.g., the teacher tells a joke, the teacher is dramatic). List at least fifteen ideas.
2. The teacher will read information to the students from *USA Today*. The students are to listen but not take notes during the reading. After the teacher completes the recitation, then the students have five minutes in which to write all the information they can recall.

The teacher can lead a discussion on the following:

Why did students recall specific bits of information?
How did the students recall ideas?
What did the teacher do that assisted the students in recalling ideas?
How could the teacher have helped the students recall more ideas?

8 Delivery

Students are encouraged to raise their hands in class to get the teacher's attention. People offer their hands in a gesture of friendship and greeting. When a teacher wants a student to talk, the teacher may give the student a sustained, direct look, point, or simply nod in the student's direction. Infants stand in front of the refrigerator and point so that the parent knows the child wants something from the refrigerator. During exam time the teacher often walks around the room to scrutinize the students. When a person is unhappy, the face and body may send nonverbal messages that indicate unhappiness to other people. An experienced gambler will often control the nonverbal signals or be "poker-faced" so other gamblers do not know how to bet. Politicians attempt to look confident, credible, composed, and yet friendly by their facial and body movements. All of these are aspects of nonverbal communication. In the public speaking context, nonverbal communication has traditionally been referred to as *delivery.* It is the point at which the speaker stands in front of the audience and begins to talk. It involves the voice, eye contact, and gestures.

It has been estimated that more than half of the emotional meaning in any social situation evolves from nonverbal messages. Although the estimates given are somewhat high, scholars and practitioners agree that much of the affective meaning a person receives from a message comes from the nonverbal component of the message. Even if a person is not visible to another (e.g., using the phone), the person's voice sends cues as to what he or she is thinking or feeling. Many people have had the experience of calling a company for information and getting a person with a monotone or harsh-sounding voice. Usually, these types of vocal tones do not encourage a person to carry on a conversation or to call back for more information.

This chapter reviews the significance of nonverbal communication, including the functions and categories of nonverbal communication, and nonverbal immediacy in the public presentation context. "Nonverbal communication is the process of a person or persons stimulating meaning in the mind of another person or persons by means of nonverbal behaviors and messages" (Richmond & McCroskey, 2000, p. 1). Therefore, nonverbal communication is the "unspoken exchange" or all the messages that individuals send or receive beyond words in the public presentation.

Significance of Nonverbal Communication

1. *Nonverbal communication is ever present.* Many communication scholars and practitioners acknowledge the fact that nonverbal communication continues even when verbal communication has ended. The idea that "one cannot not communicate," confirms the idea that nonverbal communication is ever present. People can communicate with each other nonverbally, even when they are not speaking. For example, a pause, look, or gesture often says more than words. When speaking, if the speaker uses no gestures and looks at his or her notes the entire time, the listeners get the impression that the speaker is unprepared or afraid or both.

2. *Nonverbal communication is culture specific.* All cultures have nonverbal communication. However, nonverbal behaviors may not stimulate the same meaning in one culture that they do in another. For example, the "A-okay sign" in this culture means "all's well, things are fine," or "everything is good." In other cultures the A-okay sign may stimulate a vulgar meaning in the mind of receivers. Therefore, when speaking in cultures different from that of the United States, it is important to know the various nonverbal emblems and the meanings they stimulate.

3. *Nonverbal communication may be more relevant than verbal communication.* In some speaking situations the nonverbal communication may be more important than the verbal, and in some situations the verbal may be more important than the nonverbal. Each situation is different. To determine the impact of either nonverbal or verbal communication, the context or situation must be reviewed. The unanimated speaker may use words to indicate how enthusiastic he is about the topic, but if his face doesn't indicate his interest, the listeners are not convinced. Generally, both verbal and nonverbal cues are important in the understanding of the human communication process, and listeners expect the speaker's verbal and nonverbal cues to be consistent.

4. *Nonverbal communication was the first form of communication in the history of the human species.* Before words, written communication, sign language, drum language, and so on, the human species used nonverbal messages to convey meaning. Often gestures and vocalic noises were used to convey meaning. Today, on occasion, the species still communicates this way. For example, if a person is greedily devouring a plate of barbecued ribs and another person tries to interrupt, the consumer of the food might growl or mutter and wave the intruder away.

Functions of Nonverbal Messages

Complementing. Complementing is the nonverbal function of adding to, clarifying, enriching, emphasizing, or supplementing the spoken message in the public context. For example, when a presenter says to an audience, "You are one of the best audiences I have ever spoken with," the words alone will probably be well received by the audience. However, if the words are emphasized by a pleasant, warm voice and accompanied by a smile and a positive head nod, then the message is even stronger. Consider the presenter who says to an audience, "You are one of the least interesting audiences I have ever spoken with." Again, the words alone will probably communicate the meaning to the audience. However, if the words are emphasized by a hard, unpleasant, loud voice and accompanied by a long stare on the part of the presenter, then the message is even stronger!

Contradicting. Contradicting is when the nonverbal messages are opposite to the spoken message. In other words, the nonverbal message disclaims or does not support the verbal message. Consider, for example, the couple who has been dating for several months. The woman says, "You love me, don't you?" The man says, "Sure, sure, I love you." Again, the words alone should be enough to convey the true meaning, but they often are not. The woman needs to listen and watch the nonverbal behaviors. The woman needs to hear the unsure, perhaps even questioning, tone in the man's voice and observe that while the man is expressing affection for her, he is still looking at other women!

When the spoken message is contradicted by the nonverbal message, most people tend to believe the nonverbal message. The exception to this rule is some younger children. Until about age ten to twelve, many children are more likely to believe the pure verbal message, in the literal sense. Younger children simply do not understand contradictory messages, and they tend to listen to the verbal communication.

Repeating. Nonverbal messages that restate, reinforce, duplicate, or reiterate the verbal messages serve the function of repeating. Nonverbal messages performing this function can stand alone and still represent a similar message, even if the verbal messages were not present. For example, a speaker attempting to get an audience to become quiet might say, "Please be quiet," while putting a finger to his or her lips. A student requesting help might say, "I need help with this project," while raising a hand. Either gesture (speaker signals quiet or student raising hand for help) might communicate the intended meaning in absence of the verbal, but when both the verbal and the nonverbal are present, the nonverbal gestures perform the repeating function.

Regulating.   Verbal communication is controlled, monitored, coordinated, and managed through the nonverbal function of regulating. Such regulation is accomplished primarily by nonverbal messages. These nonverbal messages can involve almost any part of the body and regulate or control the back-and-forth flow of dialogue. Some of these regulators are as follows: pointing, direct eye contact, raising or lowering speech, looking away, leaning forward, leaning back, sitting silently, pausing, touching on hand, and so on.

Often politicians know how to regulate the back-and-forth flow of interaction. A politician will pause and look at a newsperson when the politician wants the newsperson to speak. When a politician wants to "keep the floor" or continue talking, he or she will not look directly at the newsperson or pause, but keep a continuous stream of speech and use nonverbal behaviors that do not allow the newsperson to interrupt.

Substituting.   Substitution happens when the nonverbal message is delivered in place of a spoken message. Often, we will replace a verbal message with a nonverbal message because the nonverbal will communicate as effectively as, or better than, the verbal message. In public speaking, we might substitute a sustained look or pause rather than using words to make a point.

Accenting.   Nonverbal messages that highlight, stress, or enhance the spoken message serve the function of accenting. These messages can be vocalic behavior, touch, eye contact, body movement, posture, facial expression, and so on. For example, when a speaker says, "There will be *four* major points covered during this presentation," audiences tend to listen better. The word *four* is highlighted by the speaker by vocalic underlining or highlighting. Usually audiences will listen and retain more when speakers use accenting as a means to keep attention.

In conclusion, these nonverbal functions do not always occur independently. In fact, many of these nonverbal functions could occur simultaneously. It is possible to complement, repeat, and accent virtually at the same time. Many times one nonverbal function can fulfill the purpose of the source. At other times, several nonverbal functions are necessary to do so. Although some verbal messages may stand alone and communicate meaning, the meaning is often enhanced by the interaction of verbal and nonverbal components of a message.

Categories of Nonverbal Messages

Because the nonverbal component of the human communication process is critical to ongoing, effective public communication, several common nonverbal categories need to be mentioned. Therefore, each major nonverbal category follows and is briefly discussed.

Physical Appearance

As public communicators we often get "only one opportunity" to make a good first impression. Therefore, our physical appearance is critical to a successful first impression. The initial message a person sends to another person is often generated by our physical appearance. People judge others by physical appearance. If physical appearance is not acceptable, others may select not to communicate. Many aspects of physical appearance produce potential messages, such as physical features, body shape and size, height, weight, and hairstyle and color. For example, in most cultures people often make judgments about others based on body weight or height.

Dress and Artifacts

In accord with general physical appearance, dress, clothing style and type, and the artifacts or accessories with which a person adorns his or her body convey messages about the person. Dress, clothing style, and artifacts often determine whether a person will communicate with another or the type of communication that occurs. For example, if a speaker wears a tie decorated with vignettes about Bart Simpson or Winnie the Pooh, the audience may respond differently than if the speaker wears a solid black tie. When delivering a speech, avoid wearing anything that may be a distraction to the content of your speech. For example, avoid beepers, watches that may "beep," pens that you might "click" on and off, and noisy jewelry. You should also avoid having loose change or other noisy items in your pockets. Also avoid excessive cosmetics of any kind.

Rule 1.   Use appropriate dress, clothing, and current acceptable styles.

Rule 2.   Unless trying to make a point by unusual dress, always dress to suit the audience. If the audience is a conservative group, dress conservatively.

Rule 3.   Wear conservative colors such as navy, black, gray, or burgundy.

Rule 4.   Less is more. Watch everything you wear from your shoes to your accessories. Never let accessories overwhelm your appearance. When in doubt, dress simply; do not overaccessorize.

Gestures and Body Movements

The study of the communicative aspects of gestures and body movements is referred to as kinesics. This area focuses on the movement of hands, arms, legs, torso, limbs, postural cues, walking behavior, head movement, and many other gestures and movements. For example, how a person sits can send cues to another person. If the person sits with legs toward another, this may mean responsiveness. If the person sits with legs away from another, this may mean unresponsiveness. If a person leans toward the audience, he or she may be perceived as more open and responsive.

Rule 5.   Use positive gestures; negative gestures can put the audience at a distance.

Rule 6.   Use a posture that demonstrates your interest in improving relationships with your audience. Lean slightly toward the audience.

Rule 7.   Stand straight, but relaxed. Do not appear too stiff or too relaxed. Stand and look composed and in control.

Rule 8.   Keep hands out of pockets, off board, and never turn your back to your audience.

Face and Eye Behavior

The study of the communicative aspects of the face includes all facial cues such as mouth movements, lip movements, nose and cheek reactions, and eyebrow and forehead movement. Often included in facial behavior is eye behavior, which is referred to as oculesics. It is extremely difficult, often impossible, to separate oculesics from facial expression; therefore, face and eyes are often combined. In addition, many people in this culture believe that the eyes present more important nonverbal messages than do other parts of the face.

> *Rule 9.*   Give your audience your entire face and look at the audience members. Looking down or away will make the audience look down or away.
>
> *Rule 10.*   Facially, appear composed and pleasant when talking with your audience.
>
> *Rule 11.*   Look at your audience; scan the audience and environment. Do not stare at one member or above the audience. Certainly do not look down at the floor.
>
> *Rule 12.*   When first starting to speak, look at the more positive members of the audience, then move to the less positive members of your audience. This might help you reduce nervousness.

Vocal Behavior

The study of the vocal aspects of the voice is known as vocalics or paralanguage. The work in these areas includes the characteristics of the voice, uses of voice, tone, pitch, resonance, accent, dialect, and silence. A person's voice can convey to others as much information as the body, face, or eyes. For example, James Earl Jones (the voice of CNN) is often equated with power, status, strength, and credibility.

> *Rule 13.*   Use vocal variety: Avoid monotones, flat, nasal, or harsh-sounding vocalic tones.
>
> *Rule 14.*   Use warm, accepting vocal tones when speaking with your audience.
>
> *Rule 15.*   Occasionally, pause after making a major point or assertion, asking a rhetorical question, or expressing an idea so that the audience can digest the information.
>
> *Rule 16.*   Speak at a natural rate; do not speak too slowly or too quickly. Yet it is better to speak too quickly than too slowly.

Space

Proxemics is the study of the communicative aspects of space. The study of space usually includes two primary areas: personal space and territoriality. Personal space is the expandable bubble that people carry. This bubble can expand or not based on the other persons in the environment. Territoriality is how people manage the space to which they are assigned or they own. For example, how a professor arranges office furniture communicates much about the professor.

> *Rule 17.*   Move into the audience, if possible. Leave the podium or lectern behind.

> *Rule 18.*   Use movements that engage the audience. Avoid unusually wide or expansive movements that might distract the audience, unless making a point.

Touch

Haptics is the study of the communicative aspects of touch. Touch has been shown to be one of the more powerful messages transmitted in human interaction. In this culture, many people tend to be touch avoidant because of either fear of touch or fear that the touch will be misperceived by another person. For example, many teachers are hesitant to touch students in a friendly manner because the student, parent, or another teacher might misperceive the touch.

> *Rule 19.*   You can give an audience member encouragement by touching his or her hand, arm, or shoulder. Never touch elsewhere.

Environmental Cues

Environmental cues have been found to have a significant impact on human communication. The primary environmental cues that impact communication are characteristics of environment such as warmth, coldness, privacy, openness, architecture, spacial arrangements, attractiveness, color, lighting, temperature, and olfaction (smell). For example, if rooms are overly crowded, too hot, or have odors, these environmental cues can affect communication or even prevent effective communication. If an environment is too oppressive, speakers and audiences often cannot communicate as well. If an environment is properly lighted, comfortable, temperature moderated, and external odors and noises are limited, then speakers and audiences tend to communicate better with one another.

Rule 20.   Always check out the environment in which you will be presenting. Change it, if possible, to meet your needs and the audience's needs. Make the audience accessible to you.

Rule 21.   Keep the room well lit and free from distractions and bad odors.

Time

Chronemics is the study of the communicative aspects of time. The United States culture is one of the more time-conscious cultures in the world. This time orientation determines how a person perceives another person. For example, this culture is unforgiving of the person who is always late for events. In fact, people who are consistently late in this culture are stereotyped as lazy, uncaring, and selfish. This culture truly believes "The early bird catches the worm," and often much better than the worm.

Rule 22.   Begin your presentation on time; end on time. Most instructors will provide time limits (for example, four to six minutes). Prepare your speech toward the middle of the range (around five minutes so that you will not go over or under). Do not waste time looking for visual aids or note cards; have them prepared and in order before you begin.

Rule 23.   Never ever be late for a presentation, unless you are doing so for effect or the tardiness cannot be helped, such as when another speaker talks longer than his or her allotted time.

Rule 24.   If possible, leave some time for audience interaction.

Immediacy and Communication

Immediacy is the degree of perceived physical or psychological closeness between people. The concept may be best understood in terms of the immediacy principle as outlined by the person who introduced this concept into the literature, Mehrabian (1971): "People are drawn toward persons and things they like, evaluate highly, and prefer; they avoid or move away from things they dislike, evaluate negatively, or do not prefer" (p. 1). This social psychological perspective suggests that positive affect causes people to become more immediate, whereas negative affect produces reduced immediacy.

Although immediacy has received some attention from communication scholars interested in interpersonal and/or organizational communication, it has been researched primarily in the context of the college classroom. Several studies have been conducted looking at immediacy behaviors of teachers during instructional communication with their students. These studies have found nonverbal immediacy behaviors to be associated with more positive affect as well as increased cognitive learning and more positive student evaluations of teachers. This research has suggested the appropriateness of a communication principle that is the reverse of Mehrabian's social psychological principle: The more communicators employ immediate behaviors, the more others will like, evaluate highly, and prefer such communicators, and the less communicators employ immediate behaviors, the more others will dislike, evaluate negatively, and reject such communicators. We prefer to call this idea the "principle of immediate communication" (Richmond & McCroskey, 2000). There are two primary forms of immediacy: nonverbal and verbal immediacy. Nonverbal immediacy is discussed below. Verbal immediacy will be discussed in the next chapter.

It is clear from the preceding review of nonverbal behaviors in the public speaking setting that the speaker who uses more nonverbally immediate behaviors will have more positive outcomes than will the speaker who is not immediate. Nonverbal immediacy behaviors are the gestalt or all the positive nonverbal behaviors we have discussed that should be used in the public speaking context. Nonverbally immediate behaviors are the behaviors such as standing closer to your audience, leaning toward your audience, smiling, positive facial affect, direct eye contact, facing your audience, touching when needed, using positive gestures, and using appropriate temporal and environmental cues. The nonverbally immediate public speaker is one who is responsive, warm, accepting, and open to his or her audience. The nonverbally immediate public speaker is one who says in a nonverbal manner that he or she wants to talk with the audience, not talk "at" the audience.

Outcomes of Immediacy

It is clear from the review of nonverbal immediacy that positive outcomes in the public speaking setting can be stimulated by immediacy cues. For example, being verbally immediate, standing close to another, leaning toward another, smiling, having eye contact, facing another, touching, using positive gestures, and using time and smell appropriately allow one to make a favorable impression on the other person. Many of the conclusions and much of the discussion cited next come from the work of Richmond and her associates. The remainder of this section explores several outcomes of immediacy cues in public speaking settings.

Increased Liking, Affiliation, and Affect.   Mehrabian (1971), Richmond (1998), Richmond (1990), and Mottet and Richmond (1998) have confirmed that as immediacy increases, so does liking in interpersonal encounters. Mehrabian suggests that "immediacy and liking are two sides of the same coin, that is, liking encourages greater immediacy and immediacy produces more liking" (1971, p. 77). He and others have suggested that people normally communicate with those whom they like. As they communicate more with people they like, the use of immediacy can improve the affect even more. Research from many areas clearly indicates that the more a person likes another, the more they will use affirmative cues such as leaning closer, touching, mutual gaze, smiling, and nodding— all immediacy cues. On the other side of the coin, Mehrabian (1971) says that "opportunities for increased immediacy can foster greater liking" (p. 77). If one wants to be liked by another, one should use the immediacy behaviors that are likely to increase liking. For example, Mehrabian (1981) states,

> Greater liking is conveyed by standing close instead of far, leaning forward instead of back while seated, facing directly instead of turning to one side, touching, having mutual gaze or eye contact, extending bodily contact as during a handshake, prolonging goodbyes, or using gestures during a greeting that imply a reaching out toward the other person who is at a distance (p. 42).

He suggests that the above behaviors not only increase liking or affect for another but also increase the approachability of the person.

More Approachable Communication Style.   The public speaker who exhibits immediacy communication behaviors is perceived as having a more approachable communication style than the person who exhibits nonimmediacy behavior. For example, are you more likely to listen to someone who is smiling at you or someone who is frowning at you? This is a simple example, but normally out of one hundred people, at least 90 percent are more comfortable approaching the person who is smiling. If the simple distinction between smiling and frowning can make such a big difference in whether one will approach another, imagine what a cluster of immediate or nonimmediate behaviors can do. Immediacy cues not only give a speaker a more approachable communication style but also help to decrease uncertainty about the person and the situation. Often we infer how a conversation will go based on the nonverbal cues of others. Immediacy cues help to decrease uncertainty about communication situations.

More Responsiveness, Understanding, and Assertiveness.   Responsiveness is the capacity to be sensitive to the communication of others, to be seen as a good listener, to make others comfortable in communicating, and to recognize the needs and desires of others. Considerable research suggests that people who exhibit immediacy behavior are perceived as more responsive and understanding of others. Ask yourself whether you would rather communicate with a responsive person or a nonresponsive person. A responsive individual knows not only when and how to listen to another but also how to respond in a given situation. He or she knows the appropriate nonverbal and verbal communication behavior to use to improve communication. These are immediate behaviors.

Assertiveness is the ability to take a stand, defend one's beliefs, and express oneself without attacking or becoming verbally or physically aggressive. Immediate people are perceived as likely to be assertive as well as responsive.

Increased Solidarity between Participants.   Solidarity is the perception of closeness derived from similarity in sentiments, behavior, and symbols of that closeness. As immediacy increases between the speaker and his or her audience, so does solidarity; as solidarity increases, so does immediacy. We are much more likely to develop a solid relationship with a speaker who uses immediate cues with us than with one who uses nonimmediate cues. In addition, as we become closer to another, immediacy tends to increase.

Decreased Anxiety.   In most speaking situations, there is a high degree of anxiety or tension associated with the public speaking context. However, as the public speaking relationship develops, the anxiety lessens. Some of this decrease in anxiety results from verbal communication. Most of it results from nonverbal cues. Immediacy behavior tends to relax and calm another person so he or she can communicate without high anxiety. This does not mean that immediacy is the cure for anxiety; it is simply one method of alleviating tension in speaking situations.

Decreased Status Differences.   Status is the societal level of a person. The higher the difference in status between two people, the less likely the persons will communicate effectively. One proven method of reducing status differences to improve communication is to use immediacy behavior. People of higher status in organizations have learned that to communicate more effectively with subordinates, they must reduce their status without giving up the authority. Immediacy enables them to do this. A public speaker can be friendly and immediate without giving up his or her power.

Increased Perceptions of Communication Competence.   Although researchers disagree on the definition of communication competence, several communication variables emerge from the literature as characteristics normally considered necessary for a competent communicator. The most common of these are assertiveness, responsiveness, and versatility. To be perceived as competent, a speaker must be assertive, responsive, and versatile (knowing when to be assertive and when to be responsive). Immediacy behavior can be part of each of these characteristics (Richmond, 1998; Thomas, Richmond, & McCroskey, 1990). People can be assertive while being immediate. People who are responsive are definitely immediate. Finally, versatile communicators know when immediacy is appropriate and when it is not. They also have the option of using it whenever they need to. Many incompetent public speakers know what immediacy is but cannot demonstrate the behaviors when they need to. Therefore, immediacy skills help people to be perceived as more competent communicators.

Buhr, Clifton, and Pryor (1994) show that immediacy behavior enhances perceptions of some public speakers as likable, competent, trustworthy, and similar to their audiences. The authors state:

> Speaker immediacy appears to affect information processing, such that receivers rehearse more positive and neutral thoughts, and fewer negative thoughts about the speech and speaker. . . . [The nonimmediate delivery promotes more speech and speaker-relevant thoughts, [and] these thoughts are predominantly of a negative kind. This negative affect toward the speaker apparently leads to more negative thinking about the speech itself] (p. 5).

Immediacy behavior is one of the most valuable communication tools a person can have. By this point in the chapter, it may seem that immediacy is the answer to all the world's problems! Well, as with anything else, if it looks too good to be true, then it probably is. There are drawbacks associated with being immediate. The drawbacks usually are not nearly as serious as those of being nonimmediate, but they can create some problems.

Limitations of Immediacy

The first drawback of immediacy deals with perceptions. Occasionally, people mistake or misread immediacy cues for intimacy cues. You may have experienced the following. You are in a bar. Someone smiles at you and, because you want to seem friendly, you smile back. Before you can count to ten, that person is at your side asking if you would like to go home with him or her. All you did was smile! Over time, as you use immediacy behavior, you will learn when and where to use it appropriately.

The second drawback of immediacy deals with anxiety. Some people are not more relaxed or less anxious when someone is being immediate. These people like to avoid communication as much as possible. Communication avoidants may be more anxious, not less, when someone is being immediate with them. Immediacy usually increases communication, and communication avoidants want less. Therefore, their anxiety levels may increase. This is easily recognizable. If you are being immediate and someone else is not responding and seems anxious, the best thing you can do is to be less immediate. Let the other person figure out the conversational flow. Being less immediate with communication avoidants might help them be less anxious. As a speaker, you might have less eye contact with avoidants to prevent this problem.

The last drawback of immediacy could be interpreted as a positive or a negative. Immediacy promotes more communication between people. Sometimes this can be very rewarding. However, occasionally it is not. More communication requires more time. For example, the nurse who is immediate with his or her patients might find that this increases communication. This may require the nurse to spend more time with patients than is possible in a day and still carry out other duties. Therefore, one has to learn how to withdraw gracefully from a communication relationship when it is necessary to move to another one. Many people in sales are very adept at this sort of thing. They can be immediate even as they shake your hand to say good-bye.

In conclusion, the drawbacks to immediacy can create problems. However, the perceptions created in the mind of another by not being immediate are likely to be even more severe. Nonimmediate speakers are perceived by others as less friendly, less responsive, less outgoing, less likable, cold, aloof, and even hostile. Therefore, the advantages of immediacy outweigh the drawbacks.

Before we conclude this chapter, take a moment to complete Table 8.1 and get your score. The Self-Report of Immediacy Behavior (SRIB) assesses how immediate you see your communication behavior. If your behaviors are less immediate than you would like them to be, try a few of the immediacy behaviors discussed in this chapter. Select those you believe would be easy to use and see whether their use improves your communication with others. After you try two or three, try a few more until you have behaviors you feel comfortable using in speaking situations. Not everyone can use all the immediacy behaviors, so select those that are most suitable for you. The effects of immediacy do not depend on which methods you use, but on whether you do use some.

SUMMARY

Nonverbal communication is an important element in public talk. It is through gestures and facial expressions that members of the audience form an impression of who the speaker is and how interested he or she is in speaking on the chosen topic. The speaker can increase credibility and interpersonal attraction as well as homophily by paying careful attention to dress, gestures, timing, proxemics, and voice. Whereas this chapter focuses on the nonverbal elements of immediacy, the next chapter illustrates how credibility and attraction may be increased by using the proper words.

EXERCISE

Take each function of nonverbal communication and review a public speaking situation in which this function was used. Discuss the situation in detail. Discuss the corresponding outcomes for each nonverbal function.

TABLE 8.1   Self-Report of Immediacy Behavior (SRIB)

Directions: The following sixteen statements describe the ways some people behave while talking with or to others. Indicate in the space at the left of each item the degree to which the statement applies to your communication behavior. Begin each sentence with "I."

> 1 = Never
> 2 = Rarely
> 3 = Occasionally
> 4 = Often
> 5 = Very Often

_____   **1.** Use hands and arms to gesture while talking to people.

_____   **2.** Use monotone or dull voice while talking to people.

_____   **3.** Look at people while talking to them.

4. Frown while talking to people.

5. Have a tense body position while talking to people.

7. Use a variety of vocal expressions while talking to people.

8. Touch people on the shoulder or arm while talking to them.

_____   **9.** Smile while talking to people.

_____   **10.** Look away from people while talking to them.

_____   **11.** Have a relaxed body position while talking to people.

_____   **12.** Am stiff while talking to people.

_____   **13.** Avoid touching people while talking to them.

_____   **14.** Move closer to people while talking to them.

_____   **15.** Am animated while talking to people.

_____   **16.** Look bland or neutral when talking to people.

Scoring

Step 1: Add scores for items 2, 4, 5, 6, 10, 12, 13, and 16.
Step 2: Add scores for items 1, 3, 7, 8, 9, 11, 14, and 15.
Step 3: Add 44 to your total from Step 2.
Step 4: Subtract your total from Step 1 from your total from Step 3.

The total from Step 4 is your SRIB score. It will be between 16 and 80. If it is below 16 or above 80, you have made a mistake in your score.

The higher your score, the more immediate you see your communication behavior to be.

CHAPTER

9 Verbal Effectiveness (Style)

Verbal effectiveness is the degree to which a speaker can successfully communicate his or her message to the receiver using words. It is difficult for a speaker to succeed without using words effectively. The traditional name for this is *style*. As with the common definition of style, the use of language as style indicates that the words you use are a major part of how you present yourself. This chapter reviews various verbal effectiveness elements that speakers should consider employing when preparing to give a presentation. The words in a speech should have the qualities of being immediate, affinity seeking, simple, specific, clear, accurate, relevant, correct, adequate, appropriate, and vibrant.

Using Immediate Language

As discussed in Chapter 8, *immediacy* is the degree of perceived physical or psychological closeness between people. Although nonverbal immediacy has received attention from communication scholars interested in interpersonal, instructional, and organizational communication, verbal immediacy has received attention from scholars interested in the speaker's language. There are two primary forms of immediacy: nonverbal and verbal. Chapter 8 focuses on the nonverbal aspects. This chapter focuses on words. In discussing immediacy, we are concerned with what historically was called *rapport*. Rapport is a means of letting the audience know that the speaker and the listeners are getting along well—that they are "close." Such an approach helps break down the barriers that may exist between the speaker and the audience.

What people say can cause one to feel either closer to or more distant from them. Increased immediacy is produced by messages that show openness to the other, caring for the other, friendship for the other, or empathy with the other person(s). Such simple things as the use of the pronoun *we* or *us* rather than *you* or *you and I* can increase the feeling of immediacy. For example, when trying to denote verbal immediacy to a peer, you might say, "We can do this together," rather than "You should try this."

One of the most important ways of increasing immediacy in a relationship is sending verbal messages that encourage the other person to communicate. Such comments as "I see what you mean," "Tell me more," "Please continue," "That is a good idea," "This is a team effort," and "Let's talk more about this," create increased immediacy. Contrast these statements with the following comments: "Oh, shut up," "You've got to be kidding," "No way," "I thought of that," and "That is just dumb." If you were to hear any of the latter comments, would you want to communicate further? Probably not. You would not feel very close to the person who made such comments, unless it were clear he or she were joking. Of course, addressing an individual by his or her preferred name is more likely to denote immediacy than addressing one by a comment such as "Hey, you!"

Mottet and Richmond (1998) have shown that working with approach-oriented communication strategies is a much more powerful communication tool in relationship formation than are avoidance or verbally nonimmediate communication strategies. The verbal approach (AP) strategies are some of the most common strategies used by people in relationship formation. The verbal avoidance (AV) strategies are some of the most common offensive communication strategies people can employ when attempting to terminate a relationship (see Table 9.2).

Table 9.1 provides words, phrases, and ideas that help create and maintain rapport (or immediacy) with the audience. There are also their opposites, verbal avoidance items (Table 9.2).

As verbal approach increases, so does the likelihood of a positive relationship between the speaker and the audience. As verbal avoidance increases, the likelihood of a positive relationship decreases. Therefore, if you have not built affinity or liking and you use verbal avoidance statements, then you have distanced yourself from the other person and virtually guaranteed that there will be no significant relationship or that any existing relationship will be negative.

Affinity-Seeking Strategies

The process of affinity seeking is important not only in interpersonal relationships but also in public relationships. True, affinity seeking is perhaps easier in interpersonal, one-on-one, face-to-face relationships. However, verbal affinity-seeking strategies can assist people in becoming better, more effective public presenters. *Affinity seeking* is the process of getting others to like or respect the speaker. Therefore, it is essential that public presenters use some verbal affinity-seeking strategies to establish rapport and trust with an audience. The affinity-seeking strategies that follow were generated by Bell and Daly (1984). Some of the strategies have been revised by McCroskey and Richmond (1996).

TABLE 9.1   Revised Mottet and Richmond Verbal Approach/Avoidance Items

---

1. Use *ritualistic statements* by saying such things as "Good morning," "Good evening," "Hi, how are you doing?" "Take care," "This has been enjoyable," "Be careful," "I'll see you soon," "Hope to see you soon."

2. Use *self-disclosive statements* such as revealing personal stories about your life and telling the audience your thoughts, ideas, and some opinions.

3. *Express caring and appreciation* by saying such things as "I'm here for you," "I care about you," "I'm glad you invited me here," and "I value this opportunity."

4. Use statements that *address the audience's character* by saying such things as "I trust you," "I respect you," "You're dependable," "What do you think?" "How do you feel about . . . ?"

5. Use *responsive statements* with your audience, such as "I understand how you feel," "Go on, please continue," "Tell me more," "I want to listen."

6. Use *direct references and personal recognition* when communicating by remembering something from a prior conversation or presentation and referring to it; by remembering something unique about your audience; or by saying such things as "I wish you could have been there . . . ," "I thought about you when . . . ," "I remembered an idea your group suggested earlier . . . "

7. Use *praise, complimentary, and encouraging statements* with your audience such as "You look nice today," "You have a good sense of humor," "I have a lot of fun with you," and "You are a great audience, keep it up."

8. Use *communication that includes the audience* by talking about things you have in common with the audience or by talking about things you have done with your audience or members of your audience (e.g., sports, jobs, social events, attitude, beliefs, values).

9. Use *language that your audience understands*—language that does not sound superior, is not over your audience's head, or is not condescending or "talking down" to your audience.

10. Use *communication in a way that reveals that you are willing to communicate* and that you want to continue communicating by saying such things as "I'll get back to you on that issue" or "When will I hear from you again?"

TABLE 9.2   Eight Verbal Avoidance (AV) Items

1. Use discourteous and abrupt communication by interrupting or changing the subject, using inappropriate profanity, and answering an audience member's question with some curt, short, and abrupt yes/no answers.

2. Use only task-oriented communication by keeping all communication strictly business and never engaging in small talk or self-disclosure communication.

3. Use exclusionary communication by discussing topics or ideas your audience cannot relate to and topics your audience finds uninteresting; by using slang, jargon, tech talk (shoptalk) that your audience does not understand; or by talking about people and places with which your audience has little or no experience.

4. Use communication that is unresponsive by saying such things as "I don't have time now," "I'm tired," "Can you ask me later?" "I cannot answer that now. Another time, okay?"

5. Use condescending communication by saying such things as "You don't know what you're talking about," "Your ideas are stupid," "Why are you acting like that?" "You wouldn't understand," "You people should listen more," "YOU people."

6. Use hurtful, harmful, or condescending teasing and joking such as making fun of another person's clothing, weight, speech pattern, or general appearance; for example, addressing an audience of larger size people and noting that cellulite must be a number-one product of that region of the state or making bad jokes about how another group or audience pronounces words.

7. Use offensive communication by making ugly jokes and derogatory comments about the audience's ethnicity, religion, race, lifestyle, or sex.

8. Use references that fail to recognize the individual audience by not using the group's name/nickname, by mispronouncing the group's name/nickname, or by referring to the audience as "you."

Affinity-Seeking Strategies for Public Presentations

Altruism.   People attempting to get another individual to like them try to be of help. For example, the speaker might use messages that encourage other people to help or be benevolent to other people. A classic example is when speakers ask an audience to give to the United Way or support the Salvation Army.

Comfortable Self.   The person attempting to get another to like him or her acts comfortable in the setting, comfortable with him or herself, and comfortable with the other person(s). Often speakers will make comments that are intended to put the speaker and audience at ease. A classic example is when speakers begin with "my fellow Americans."

Conversational Rule Keeping.   People attempting to get another individual to like them follow closely the culture's rules for how people are to socialize with one another by demonstrating cooperation, friendliness, and politeness. These people work hard at giving relevant answers to questions, saying the "right thing," and acting interested and involved in what others may have to contribute. Often speakers will agree with audience members' opinions or tease with audience members to put them at ease. A classic example is when a speaker verbally banters back and forth with the audience on a few issues.

Dynamism.   Here the speaker attempts to get an audience to like him or her by presenting him or herself as a dynamic, interesting speaker both verbally and nonverbally. Verbally, the speaker uses active, dynamic language; nonverbally, the speaker is active and lively.

Elicit Audience's Disclosures.   The speaker who uses this strategy encourages members of the audience to express views, opinions, and feelings, as time permits.

Facilitate Enjoyment.   In this strategy, the speaker uses entertaining stories, tells appropriate jokes, talks about interesting topics, says funny things, and tries to make the environment conducive to enjoyment.

Listening.   In this strategy, the speaker pays close attention to what the audience members have to contribute. The speaker can then respond more appropriately, ask questions of clarification, and respond with ideas or concepts the audience members raise.

Openness.   In this strategy, the speaker is open about him or herself. Speakers disclose information about their backgrounds, interests, experiences, and viewpoints.

Optimism.   Here speakers attempting to get an audience to like them present themselves as positive individuals. Speakers avoid complaining about things, talking about depressing topics, and being critical of themselves and others.

Present Interesting Self.   The speaker presents him or herself as a person who would be interesting to know. For example, he or she highlights past accomplishments and positive qualities, emphasizes things that make him or her especially interesting, expresses unique ideas, and demonstrates knowledge and competence.

Self-Concept Confirmation.   Speakers attempt to get audience members to demonstrate respect for them and help the audience members feel good about themselves. For example, the speaker treats the audience members as very important persons, gives compliments, says only positive things about the audience, and views what the audience says as very important.

Similarity or Homophily.   In this strategy, the speaker tries to make the audience think that they are similar in attitudes, beliefs, values, interests, preferences, and personality. He or she expresses views that are similar to the views of the audience, agrees with what the audience has to say, and points out ideas and things that the two have in common.

Trustworthiness.   Speakers using this strategy present themselves as trustworthy, reliable, and honest. They emphasize their responsibility, reliability, fairness, dedication, honesty, and sincerity. They also maintain consistency in their stated beliefs and behaviors, fulfill any commitments made to the audience or an individual, and avoid false fronts by acting natural at all times.

The process of a speaker getting audience members to like him or her has its greatest impact in the early stages of the presentation. These strategies provide many opportunities for a speaker, within the first minute or two, to gain a rapport and responsive nature with the audience. Not every person is comfortable with all the strategies. You can choose those that would work best for you with different audiences and speaking situations. Using affinity-seeking strategies cannot hurt you; it can only help your presentation and rapport with your audience, unless you are putting on a false front.

Other Important Qualities of Language in the Speech

Certainly immediacy and affinity seeking are primary aspects of the overall goal of language in the speech. Although examples of other aspects have been discussed as part of immediacy or affinity seeking, they should also be mentioned individually. The language should be simple, specific, clear, accurate, relevant, correct, adequate, appropriate, and vibrant.

Simple, Not Complex Language.   If you have ever heard two experts on computers talking, you may have wondered whether you were listening to an entirely different language. When terms such as *CPUs*, *RAMs*, *gigabytes*, and others are used in a speech, they need to be explained. If there are too many of these terms within a speech, only those individuals who already know what you are saying will continue to listen.

Specific, Not Abstract Language.   Although abstractions may be used when discussing philosophy, metaphysics, and the like, nonspecific language makes it difficult for listeners to follow the speaker's ideas. In addition, audience members feel the tendency to "fill in" their own notions when listening to abstractions. In fact, abstractions do not have to be complex. For example, in talking about your dog, you may want to discuss the dog according to its breed, size, sex, and age. There is a substantial difference between talking about "my dog" and "my eight-year-old black cocker spaniel."

Clear Language.   Just as you should avoid computer jargon and the jargon of other fields when you speak so that you may be clearer, also consider the use of metaphors, analogies, and examples. Descriptive terms also engage the listener better than the merely technical phrasing. "When I saw *Saving Private Ryan*, I not only felt that I could hear and feel the thump of the bullets hitting the men's chests, I felt that I could feel the heartbeat and the shortened breath as each man engaged the enemy on the hill." A sentence such as this one provides a descriptive and clear feeling of what the movie viewer felt while watching it.

Accurate Language.   To be accurate it is necessary to develop a strong vocabulary. Although many words may sound as though they mean the same thing, they obviously do not. Consider the words for *speak: say, entice, persuade, seduce, humiliate, compliment, surrender, negotiate, argue.* Certainly there are many more. Each has its own unique meaning and is used in a certain context. For example, we might say that a drill sergeant humiliated a soldier, but we would hardly say that a sergeant seduced or enticed a recruit.

Relevant Language.   As has been mentioned, the effective speaker should avoid street language and what has been described as mall talk. Saying "like, you know" or "next" and using such terms repeatedly is simply taking up silence. Silence in a speech, at appropriate times, is perfectly acceptable. Recently, the words *actual* and *actually* have also become commonplace as filler.

Correct Language.   The speaker should take special care to use correct grammar when speaking in public. As has been mentioned, incorrect grammar harms the speaker's credibility.

Adequate Language.   Someone giving directions to a person whose first language is something other than English may repeat exactly what he or she said but more slowly and louder. More often than not, this method does not fulfill the needs of the listener. Instead, learn to say the same thing in more ways that one. When asked to repeat a statement, ask the audience member whether he or she wants an exact repeat or would prefer for you to say it in other words.

Appropriate Language.   Radio and television have added some words to their vocabularies over the past few years. However, when speaking in public, avoid cursing and sexual terms, as well as ethnic and sexist jokes. If the speaker decides to make fun of someone, it should be him or herself.

Vibrant and Vivid Language.   The words in the speech should demonstrate that the speaker is alive and the speech is living. Using the same words over and over again has the same kind of effect as a monotone vocal inflection. The people in the audience begin thinking "blah, blah, blah."

Individual Differences

To some extent, language differences are referred to as style because each person is different. Individuals have their own styles. This can be seen in how people dress, in what topics are interesting to various people, in the brand names that people buy. It also can be heard in the words people use. This section focuses on three major differences among people.

Self-Disclosure

In this culture, some people self-disclose more information, with longer duration and with more intimate topics, than do others. Moreover, self-disclosing people are less guarded and more honest about revealing negative information about themselves. However, less self-disclosing people tend to reserve their most intimate disclosures only for those with whom they are close. Some people do not self-disclose much negative information about themselves to anyone.

Language Use

As noted earlier, the language people use both constructs and reflects their perceptions of reality. Thus, much research in recent years has sought to determine the effects of certain word usage on perceptions of the sexes. This body of scholarship has examined the use of particular nouns, verbs, and pronouns and found that some do indeed affect how we perceive men and women. Studies have found females to be referred to more frequently than males by informal terms (first names or nicknames); referred to more often in terms of the men with whom they are associated rather than by their own identity (Joe's wife, Mr. Smith's little girls); and identified more than men as sex objects (chick, fox, doll, babe, and so on). Therefore, when addressing audiences speakers always need to keep the language professional and inclusive of both sexes, without being derogatory. Both men and women should be referred to by their professional titles, rank, or experience.

Studies have found that women, more so than men, use more euphemisms (substituting more acceptable or polite terms for embarrassing terms). A female might say, "He is intellectually challenged," whereas a man might say, "He is stupid." Women often use more emotional terms such as *wonderful, great, how nice,* and *I just love that idea* than do men. Men may not make note of ideas by attaching emotional terms. Men are more likely to say, "Good idea, let's move forward." Women often use more intensifiers than do males. For example, women might use the term *anorexic* whereas men might use the term *skinny* or *fragile*.

When speaking to an audience, both men and women need to employ generic pronouns, unless the speaker is talking about a specific person. When the gender-specific term *him* is used for all references, it excludes half your audience, women. When the gender-specific term *her* is used for all references, it excludes half your audience, men. In order to be fair and equal, it is appropriate for both men and women speakers to say such things as "he or she," "her or him," "they," "society," "the population," and so on. In conclusion, regardless of one's biological sex, it is wise to avoid the use of the masculine or feminine terminology, which the use of generic terms is specifically designed to avoid in the first place.

Finally, people tend to use different verbs in reference to females and males. For men, verbs are generally expressed in the active voice. For women, verbs are more often expressed in the passive voice. Talking about Susan and Jim going to the store, for example, one is likely to say, "Jim took Susan to the store" (an active verb, *took*), or "Susan was taken to the store" (a passive verb, *was taken*) as opposed to "Susan rode to the store with Jim."

Subject Matter

As already noted, men and women differ in the types of information they disclose to others and language usage. On a more basic and less intimate level, the two sexes also differ relative to the types of topics with which they most frequently begin conversations. These differences occur in both same-sex and opposite-sex interactions. The results of these differences are still determined by the specific roles assigned to females and males by society. When women address other women, the most likely subjects they will discuss are men, clothing, other women, movies, books, and careers. When men address other men, the most likely subjects they will discuss are business, money, politics, sports, and other amusements. Because of the differences of subject matter, when women address men and men address women, it is as though they are speaking in a foreign language. Often men put ideas into sports metaphors, whereas women use shopping metaphors. In opposite-sex dyads, when women initiate conversation with men, they are most likely to discuss men, other women, and perhaps professional issues. When males initiate conversation with females, they are most likely to discuss sports or business.

Again, individuals are still influenced by societal and cultural rules about their expected roles. Therefore, in public speaking, you need to adapt to your audience and use subject matter all can relate to, whether it is sports, shopping, careers, money, or politics.

SUMMARY

As a public speaker, you must be able to adapt to your audience, encompass all in your presentation, use appropriate affinity-seeking strategies, and use appropriate language and subject matter. The public speaker who follows the strategies in this chapter is more likely to be successful than the one who does not. In addition, the speaker's language should be simple, specific, clear, accurate, relevant, correct, adequate, appropriate, and vibrant.

CHAPTER

10 Gathering Materials for the Talk

133

Although most speakers already have enough research to deliver a speech, the first-time speaker may lack such information. Several years ago, the average student would go to the large, green books in the school library for the first source. These books, the Reader's Guide to Periodical Literature, provided an index of materials found in popular magazines on popular topics. This guide is beneficial for few speeches that involve a great deal of substance. This is because most of the articles found in this index are short and provide little except introductory information. Such popular sources may be found in listings on disk or on Internet sources, but the criticism is the same. When an index lists a short article (one page or less), the information is of value to the speaker only for background material. What the average student neglected to consider first was his or her own knowledge.

There is usually a specific reason why a student selects a topic for a speech. One of the reasons should be that the student already knows something about the topic. One clear example of one who did not know about his subject was a student who gave a speech on the Peace Corps back in the 1960s. Throughout the entire speech, the student pronounced it as the "Peace *Corpse*." Another student answered a question about a speech on Powder Puff Auto Repair (women taking care of their automobiles). She was asked how often the air should be changed in one's tires. She responded that it should be done about every six months. Obviously these are extreme examples. Certainly there should be a significant difference between what one knows about the topic before beginning research on the speech and the delivery of the speech, but the speaker should make a special effort to talk about something about which he or she already has some knowledge.

Once the speaker has made some mental notes about his or her knowledge about the topic, he or she should begin the process of gathering materials. Just as in writing a paper, the two mistakes made most often are to research too little or too much. One must know when to stop as well as how to start. We begin our discussion in this chapter with traditional printed materials.

Printed Materials

Generally speaking, printed materials are considered highly credible sources for presentations. There are three reasons for this: (1) Several other people (editors, reviewers, readers) decided that most printed materials should be published; (2) the material can be found by someone else because it exists in an easily accessible form; and (3) such materials often provide additional sources of information.

Books

In today's world, most libraries have computerized listings of books on particular topics. The system will typically allow you to look under "subject" and find most of the books that you might need. However, this is not a particularly good source to find books for most speeches. The reason is that most books are two or three years out of date when they are published. It simply takes that long to publish a book. In addition, the length of a book makes it difficult for students to find the exact material they may need from any one source. In addition, books that appear in grocery and discount stores are mass marketed for the general public and are not specific enough for most speeches. Some students have tried to use books they have at home. This is another bad idea. Why would those books be representative of the available material? For the most part, then, eliminate this possibility. If you do use books from home, use the table of contents and the index to limit your scope. Otherwise, you may be reviewing too much useless information.

Magazines

A magazine may be a good place to start, although magazines are unlikely to be a good place to end. Most, but not all, magazine articles provide a general background of the topic. This may help you establish a more specific topic, but these articles would probably not be your most important source. For such general sources, the *Reader's Guide to Periodical Literature* may well be a good place to start. Look under topics and read each title to determine whether it meets your needs. Also look at the front, where many libraries mark the guide, to indicate which journals they have. Many students have discovered twenty or thirty articles in the guide only to find that their libraries have only ten of them. This is a bad use of time when your time is limited.

Once you have found enough to give you a background, make certain that you write down at least the title of the publication (magazine), the month and year, the author (if there is one), the title of the article, and the page numbers. For weekly magazines such as *Newsweek* and

Time, you will need to write the specific date. This careful preparation can save you much time. It is quite irritating to return to the library simply because you forgot to record enough information. Also note that certain magazines have higher credibility than others, depending on your audience for the speech. Part of the reason for this is that some magazines have editorial biases. For example, one of today's most popular magazines is *Modern Maturity*. You should note that this magazine is published by the American Association of Retired Persons. The magazine usually takes positions that the managers of the organization believe will be of benefit to the aging. A magazine such as *Reader's Digest* is often considered a low-credibility source because it is, in fact, a digest. That is, it contains brief, edited versions of longer papers, articles, and books.

A subcategory of magazines is what college professors refer to as journals. Journals are periodicals, usually published quarterly, written by college professors, which provide very detailed information about specific topics. There are usually no pictures, charts, or diagrams in these articles. Journals do contain quite detailed information about academic and nonacademic topics. Two that you have probably heard quoted are the *New England Journal of Medicine* and the *Journal of the American Medical Association (JAMA)*. Because there is much greater attention given to medical and health-care problems today, many television and radio stations quote from these two highly respected journals. When using journals, it is important for you to check their credibility. One way is to look at the front of the journal and determine who publishes it. The more respectable journals in any discipline are published by a professional association from that field. For example, *Communication Monographs* and *Communication Education* are two journals that publish research in the field of communication; they may contain articles about public speaking. These journals are published by the National Communication Association (NCA). Articles published in professional journals are generally highly credible sources in that area.

To find articles about your topic, you will need to use an index. Specialized indexes can be used just like you use the *Reader's Guide to Periodical Literature*. For whatever time frame you are seeking information, you then go to a specialized index. Let us say, for example, you want to find out about the effectiveness of smaller size classrooms in college. You might find the *Education Index*. Look at the latest one, which will be small and paperback. Look up *class size*. If you find nothing, look for associated terms such as *student–teacher ratio* or *size* or *classes*. If you still find nothing, go back one issue of the index, and continue this process until you find enough information. However, most often begin with the latest issue because that is the most up-to-date information. Unlike books, most articles are only a few months or a year out-of-date.

Newspapers

The primary advantage to newspapers as a source of information is that they are current. Despite some reporters' views to the contrary, however, newspapers are not particularly any more objective than are some other sources. When you use a newspaper as a source, pay particular attention to where the information is located in the paper. The front page examines the major news of the day, but some papers now have a section on the front page entitled (and usually marked as such) "commentary." This means that this is one writer's opinions about actual events in the news. The editorial pages are all opinions. When reading editorial pages, you need to realize the biases of the writer. Your college library will probably have some local newspapers as well as the *Wall Street Journal*, the *New York Times*, *USA Today*, and the *Washington Post*. Although generally well respected, these papers also have biases. Some instructors consider *USA Today* to be a newspaper version of *Reader's Digest*, because the paper provides brief articles whereas some other papers provide more expanded versions.

The *Wall Street Journal* has less biased information about stocks, companies, and the stock market than it has about politics. The *Journal* often sees political issues from the viewpoint of the economy, especially from the viewpoint of those who are more wealthy in society—in other words, that of most of its subscribers. The *New York Times* and the *Washington Post* most commonly see issues from what is called "the beltway perspective." That is, they look at issues from an eastern, urban view. Newspapers in Cleveland, St. Louis, Dallas, Atlanta, and Los Angeles may have quite different views on the same topics. Indeed, the relevance of certain topics is likely to be different. This is a good reason to look at some of your local or regional newspapers in addition to sources that are better known nationally. Most libraries will have an index to the *New York Times*. The primary advantage of a newspaper, then, is that an article will probably be only a day or so out-of-date.

Almanacs and Other Yearbooks

Let us assume that you have almost completed your research, but that you need a <u>fact</u> that will make your speech more credible. An almanac may be the first place to go. The information contained in almanacs is about the same, regardless of which one you use. Some, however, have better indexes and tables of contents than do others. You may find the major league records for home runs as well as the population of Nebraska. You may find a list of the colleges that are located in Pennsylvania. The variety of information is quite diverse.

Almanacs are more general sources of facts. If you need a more specific fact, such as suicides by age group, you can use the *Statistical Abstract of the United States*, published by the U.S. Department of Commerce. Other resources include *Facts on File Yearbook*, *The Guinness Book of World Records*, and the *Book of Lists*. If you are seeking even more specific information, you may go to various organizations' publications. These books are available for movies, music, and sports. Most professional organizations have directories of their members. This might be a good way to check the background of someone who wrote an article in a journal, for example. Associations such as the American Sociological Association, the American Psychological Association, and the Modern Language Association have directories, which most often contain information about whom their members are, what degrees they have, when they finished their degrees, and what rank they hold in college.

For better-known writers, background information can be found in various who's who publications. *Who's Who in America* is one of the better known. Individuals from a variety of fields can be found in this periodical directory. The *Directory of American Scholars* may be the most helpful in looking for college professors. Many different fields and regions of the country have such publications. The information in these citations is usually more complete than is a directory of a particular association.

Quotation Books

Several books contain quotations. *Bartlett's Familiar Quotations*, the *Oxford Dictionary of Quotations*, and the *Speaker's and Toastmaster's Handbook* provide a number of these more famous quotations. To find a quote applicable to your topic, you may use the <u>index</u> at the end of each of these books and look under <u>your topic</u> or <u>synonyms</u>. In the rare event that you need to use a poem in particular, you may go to the *Poetry Index*. You should use this index similarly to how you use any other index. The *Poetry Index* provides books and page numbers where a poem may be found about your topic.

Specialized Dictionaries and Encyclopedias

It is not highly recommended to use those sources you may have used in high school, such as *Webster's Dictionary* or the *World Book Encyclopedia*. Just as *USA Today* and *Reader's Digest* are meant for the general reader, these sources are too general for your purpose. Most colleges, for example, have more specific sources such as the *Encyclopedia of the Social Sciences*, the *Physician's Desk Reference*, the *Dictionary of American History*, and the *Encyclopedia of Science and Technology*. These sources are used just as you would use any other dictionary or encyclopedia. The topics are covered in alphabetical order.

Government Documents

The U.S. Government Printing Office publishes a number of books every day about what the government is doing. Most committee reports from Congress are available. If your school is fortunate enough to be a repository for government documents, you can find all of these documents there. Some of these sources include the *Index to U.S. Government Periodicals*, the *American Statistics Index*, the *Monthly Catalog of United States Government Publications*, the *United States Reports*, and the *Congressional Record*.

The first three are indexes. The *United States Reports* is a record of Supreme Court decisions. This, and other legal publications, are sometimes difficult to read. To find other sources on legal matters, however, one would probably need to "shepherdize" the cases. This method is essentially an indexing method used in legal cases and law journals. To use these materials, you may want to obtain assistance from a librarian who works in that section of the library.

Many people believe that the *Congressional Record* is an official record of what has been said in Congress; you should note, however, that there is substantial editing of these materials and that some information contained therein is never stated before Congress. One advantage to these publications, though, is that they provide a governmental perspective as opposed to journalistic or academic views.

Pamphlets and Brochures

Another type of printed material that is used for public speaking is the pamphlet or brochure. For the most part these publications are printed for particular organizations. Your college probably has a "recruiting" brochure for students. When you go to your doctor's office, you probably find pamphlets about certain diseases, most often those of the doctor's specialty. A cardiologist may have a brochure about heart disease. A gynecologist may have a brochure about preventing sexually transmitted diseases.

Some brochures are weighted toward information. Others are no more than propaganda about a particular issue; that is, they are highly biased. Most people would not argue that all of us should reduce our fat intake. However, a number of people would argue with the National Rifle Association that we have a constitutional right to own guns. It is important to check the brochure to see who is responsible for publishing it. Then it is important to discover information about that organization or person before deciding to use it.

Computer Databases

Many students today prefer to find information on the computer at home rather than to take a trip to the library. Certainly computers have made information retrieval less complex, faster, and more convenient. However, much of the information is less credible than what is found in a library. Therefore, you should be careful about using Web sites to gather data. Much of the information in the library is also available on the Internet. You may have access to many of your library's indexes through the Internet. Your library's version of the *Index to the Social Sciences* found on the shelves and what is available on the computer are the same. The same is true with other indexes. *ERIC*, for example, is a source used to find information about education. Many of the papers in this index have not been published; they may, therefore, be more up-to-date but less credible because they have not been through the review and editorial process that a journal article goes through.

Most students are aware that they can simply plug in a word or two to a "find" or "search" command at an Internet site such as America Online. Most often these sources provide hundreds of thousands of sites. Your ability to be as specific as possible will assist you in undertaking this task. Unfortunately, some sites are more credible than others. If, for example, you wanted to know the Academy Award winners, you might go to www.Oscar.com. Because this is an official site, your information will probably be accurate. As you know, though, anyone can open a Web site. For this reason, some teachers do not allow information directly drawn from a Web site; check with your instructor. If you are seeking information about a specific author or researcher, you might type in that person's name. Amazon.com will provide you information about what that author has published as well as books about him or her. If you know that the person is a professor and teaches at a certain university, you may go to the university's Web site, then look under faculty. Some faculty list entire bibliographies of their works. Some journals' articles are also published in their entirety on the Web site for the journal or the professional association that publishes the journal.

Let us assume that you have chosen media literacy as a topic. Generally, those involved in this topic are concerned about the effects of the mass media, especially television and the Internet, on children. You might be the advocates of media literacy as media consumer advocates. When your Internet provider asks for a topic, you list "media literacy." In the America Online version, there are 215 sites listed. Each of the sites lists its name, a sentence or so about what is in it, and the percentage of people who open to that site. The first two are the New Mexico Media Literacy Projects and the Center for Media Literacy. The first indicated that 100 percent "click it on." The second indicated 98 percent. This means that both of these sites are popular. It does not necessarily mean anything else. Just as one would evaluate sources from books, such as who published the book, we must do the same with Internet sources. Remember that sources are also advocates. An additional problem with Internet sites is that they are often trying to sell you something. Once you find the information that you need, though, you can download it or print it out. We advocate that you read or download first before you decide whether to print it. You may want to see, for example, how many pages there will be. Some sources are thousands of pages. The other advantage of downloading is that some sources contain visual materials that you may transfer to PowerPoint software.

Interviews and Surveys

It may be an advantage for the speaker to create his or her own information for the speech. Perhaps the leading expert on your topic is on your campus or in your community. Perhaps your topic is about an issue on campus for which there is no published or computer information. Two methods are often used to determine information in situations in which no one seems to have collected it before. These methods are interviews and surveys.

Interviews

Interviews typically involve the face-to-face interactions of two people in which one of them is primarily asking questions and the other is answering questions. Of course, they take place in a number of everyday situations. When you interview for a job, the employer asks most of the questions, and you provide most of the answers. The interviewer's purpose is to determine whether you are the best candidate for the job. Many companies have annual or semiannual reviews in which the boss asks questions of the subordinates to determine which ones should receive a higher pay raise. Barbara Walters and other television personalities interview stars to relate something about them that most of us do not already know. However, the purpose of an interview for the public speaker is to gain information that is not easily available. For example, you might interview the sheriff of your county to find out about local crime statistics. The local superintendent of schools can provide information about the budget for education.

Preparation for the Interview.   You will need to undertake some background research prior to telephoning your expert. Try to find out as much information as you can for your speech before calling. Then establish some general and specific questions for which you need answers. Find out as much as you can about the expert before going to the interview. This information is often available in the local newspaper. You may try to get several different interviews, with people who have differing perspectives. It is probably best, though, not to use two opposite viewpoints. You should phone the office of the individual to ask when you can meet for an interview. If an hour is available, you should ask for that much time and explain the reason for your meeting. If the expert is quite busy, you may ask whether he or she has e-mail or a Web site. If you send your questions through e-mail, you have written responses to your questions.

Planning Your Interview.   Some basic ground rules are good to start.

- Arrive a few minutes ahead of time.
- Wait patiently, perhaps looking over your notes.
- Be friendly.
- Tell the receptionist who you are and why you are there.
- Introduce yourself to the interviewee, and shake hands.

There is a four-step process of interviewing known as *FLOW.* The first step is the *focus.* This is the beginning in which you try to establish some rapport. Remind the interviewee of your topic and where you are from. Sometimes little comments, such as "I'm from Nevada," help to start the conversation. The respondent may say that he or she is also from Nevada or was recently in Las Vegas. The interviewer may begin talking about when he or she took public speaking. It is also important to be dressed appropriately, maintain eye contact, and ask whether it is all right to take notes or to use a tape recorder.

The second step is the *lead-in.* You should provide a general outline of what your questions will be. You may want to explain the point of your speech, who is in the audience, and why you chose this person to interview. The third step is the organized step. This is the body of your interview. You should have your questions in order; however, you might remember that the expert may answer your third question when you ask the first. If this happens, do not repeat the question. If the interviewer says he or she has some written materials that you may use, write a note and remember to ask about those materials before you leave. You should form your questions in different ways. Do not say, "What about so-and-so?" Instead, say, "Tell me what this community has done to reduce crime in the past four years." Use the form of address, Mr., Dr., or Ms., unless the individual has told you to do otherwise. You might keep a close watch on your time so as not to go past the time you have been given. At the conclusion, ask whether there is anything else you need to know.

The final step is the *wrap-up.* You should briefly summarize what you have found out. If you plan to use a quote, read it to the interviewee in the event that it is inaccurate or he or she wants to change it, even if ever so slightly. You should thank him or her, shake hands, and leave the office, remembering those written materials. When you leave the receptionist's area, another thank you is appropriate. Also send a thank-note within a week, perhaps explaining how your speech went.

Surveys

Let us suppose that you arc advocating that your campus have a radio station on its Web site. This issue may have come forward before, but no one knows how the students in general feel about it. You may want to do a survey. However, it is important to remember that surveys are, in fact, quite complex (Stacks & Hocking, 1999). You will need to get a good *sample*. That is, you should not just ask your friends or people who are in your major. You may select several different places on campus to obtain your sample. A sample means that you want the people you talk with to be good examples of the overall view of the campus. You must prepare questions very carefully, in an unbiased way.

Recording Your Information

Let us say that you have some information from each of the types of research that we have mentioned. You now need to decide which parts of what you have learned might be helpful to the content of your speech. You will probably need the largest size of index cards to record your information. First, you should write or type *source cards* (see Figure 10.1). Here you should provide all of the information you need to find the source in the library or on the computer again. For the other sources you should provide where you obtained the information, the date, the name of a person interviewed, the location of surveys. In short, you should record who, where, and when. If you think about it, this is what a bibliographical reference does. You may also want to record the Library of Congress or Dewey Decimal system number in case you need to find the book again. If information is from the computer, record the *exact* Web site. Also assign a letter of the alphabet to the source. You will probably not have more than ten to fifteen sources for a speech. Your instructor will usually tell you the minimum number, but you will probably need more than the minimum.

Once you have recorded all of your source cards, you begin the task of recording your *informational cards.* (see Figure 10.2). There are several methods of doing this, depending on what information you want to record and how much there is. If you are using a long article, you need several cards for each source. Your source cards will be numbered consecutively using the alphabet and a number; for example, you may have A-1, A-2, and A-3.

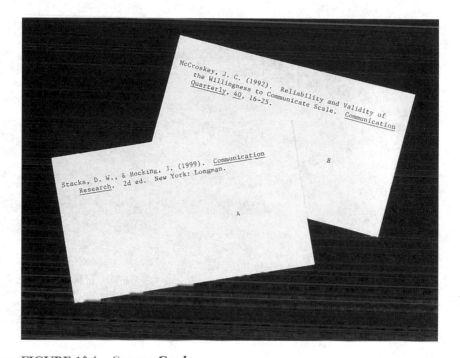

FIGURE 10.1   Source Cards

Stacks, D. W., & Hocking, J. E. (1999). *Communication research.* 2d ed. New York: Longman.

Books and lengthy articles are probably handled in this way. You may want to photocopy the pages of a book or the entire article. You then highlight the information on your photocopied copy. You can then simply "cut and paste" the information onto a card, mark it —B-1—and go to the next one. You should not place more than one piece of information per card. Make certain that you place the page number of the information on the card. If you are simply using biographical information about an author from *Who's Who in America*, you may want to write only that piece of information on the card: "James Brown is professor of history at Cambridge University." The same is true if you want to record one bit of statistical information from an interview: "Jackson County's robberies decreased from 43 to 37 between 1995 and 2000."

You should probably have at least five source cards and at least thirty informational cards when you begin to prepare for even a short speech. The next task is to decide how to use this information in the speech. In

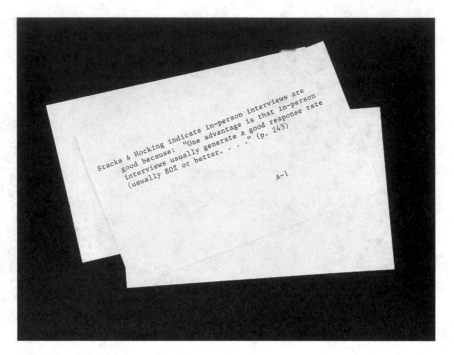

Stacks & Hocking indicate in-person interviews are good because: "One advantage is that in-person interviews usually generate a good response rate (usually 80% or better. . . ." (p. 243)

A-1

FIGURE 10.2   Informational Cards

Chapter 11, we discuss how a speaker can first determine which cards to use and which to discard. This is an especially difficult task because most speakers want to use all of the information they have found.

SUMMARY

The essence of a speech is its content. There are several ways to find information for the content of your speech. Printed sources, such as books, articles in magazines and journals, pamphlets and brochures, and special dictionaries and encyclopedias generally have high credibility. Some more popular sources should be avoided. Information is also available on the Internet, but it should be viewed more skeptically. A speaker may collect his or her own information through interviews and surveys when both the situation and time allow for it. Information needs to be recorded in a manner so that it can be found again, if necessary. Once you have developed all of the information for your speech, you must decide whether to use all of it, and if so, how.

CHAPTER

11 Using Verbal Material in Public Talk

Once you have gathered the materials for the speech from a variety of sources, it is important to decide how to use them in the speech. These materials, often referred to as *supporting materials*, form the substance of your talk. They help the speaker substantiate what he or she is saying. By using supporting materials, the speaker demonstrates that the information in the speech is based on more than experience or opinion.

There are several different types of supporting materials including facts, statistics, testimony, examples, demonstrations, narratives, and humor. Each of these materials is what Aristotle referred to as *evidence*. In informative speeches the evidence has two purposes: (1) to increase the credibility of the speaker and (2) to validate the speaker's claims. However, in persuasive discourse, evidence assists the credibility of the speaker, validates the speaker's claims, and is a strong factor in whether the audience will change in accordance with the speaker's views.

The Importance of Balance

One of the most important features of an effective speech is that the types of supporting materials used are balanced. A good speaker would not try to use only statistics throughout the speech, nor would he or she tell only a few stories and call it a speech. The various types of supporting materials that follow should be balanced for effectiveness, interest, curiosity, and purpose.

Facts

In today's world, especially if you watch daytime talk shows on television, you wonder whether there is such a thing as a fact. These programs, as well as commentary on many news programs, demonstrate that unsubstantiated opinions are often the substance of popular television. Nevertheless, we all know that some opinions are better than others. For example, we may pay more attention to a psychiatrist who has written a book about a particular problem of a guest on a talk show than we do to the audience member who says the guest should leave the country. We know that the audience member is less qualified about psychology.

We know that a physician can help us with our acid reflux problem more so than a colleague of ours can. Some opinions are better than others because of training, education, and experience. When opinions are verifiable by a number of sources who report them consistently, they become facts. Thus, a fact must be information that can be determined to be true or false. For information to be fact, there must be agreement among credible sources who have arrived at the same conclusion.

Finally, a fact must be reliable; that is, it was true two years ago and it is still true. If we asked experts about the fact today and tomorrow, they would agree both times about the nature of the fact. *Facts* are individual pieces of information. We know that information can be determined to be a fact, or it can be inaccurate. Otherwise, it is only an opinion. Which of the following can we determine to be facts?

- George Washington was the first president of the United States of America.
- The major league home run record for one season is held by Roger Maris.
- Less than 80 percent of registered voters actually vote.
- *Saving Private Ryan* is a better movie than *Titanic.*
- Maya Angelou is a country singer.
- Thomas Jefferson was the first president of the United States of America.

We know that the first statement is factual. George Washington was the first president. We know that the second statement is false. Roger Maris had 61 home runs in only one year (in 1961). In 1998, that record was surpassed by both Sammy Sosa of the Chicago Cubs and Mark McGuire of the St. Louis Cardinals. How can we make the Maris statement factual? We can say that Maris held the record from 1961 to 1998, or we can say that he still holds the record for the American League.

We can find statistics to support our statement about the voting habits of the American public. This is a factual statement. The movie comparison is a matter of opinion. It is not a fact. It is not false. Expert moviegoers might disagree. Each may have his or her own reasons for choosing one movie over the other. Maya Angelou is a writer, not a country singer. We know that Thomas Jefferson was the third, not the first, president. But how do we determine facts for issues in our speeches? How do we use facts in the speech?

We determine what the facts are by finding them in sources. For example, if we need to determine the background of an author of an article, we may search in directories, *Who's Who*, and information in the article itself. As has been mentioned, the speaker may want to say: "Dr. Joseph Brown, a professor of zoology at Emory University . . ." This is a method of footnoting your source within the speech. We may also need to find facts about dates, definitions, backgrounds. At times, too, we need factual information in the form of statistics.

Statistics

Whereas some would say that statistics are simply a type of fact, others might say that statistics are at the center of a liar's evidence. Statistics do not always generate the same credibility as do facts, *per se*. Statistics are not based on observations but on *probabilities* of observations. Statistics may be used to make statements about past, present, or future states of events, people, phenomena, behavior. Statistics are available in raw numbers. This includes figures such as the population of a given state in a certain year. Of course, this is actually an *estimate*. The number represents approximately how many people resided in that state that year.

In addition, statistics are available based on other sets of probabilities. These are statistics that are based on a sample, which project that the entire population will have a similar perspective. A *sample* is a group within the entire population being studied. This is called *inferential statistics* because an inference is being made to the entire population, based on the sample. When these projected numbers are used, the writer often states an *error factor*. Although the issue is somewhat more complex than this, the error factor in general tells us what the chances are that the sample does *not* represent the population. An error of .05, for example, means there is a 5 percent chance that the sample may not be representative of the population. An error of less than (<) .01 means that there is less than 1 percent probability than the same results would occur through chance. In medical studies, very low errors are needed (i.e., .001); in most social science studies, a .01 or .05 is used. Any study that reports a .20 error is not very useful. Of course, an error of .50 would mean a fifty/fifty chance, which is not very accurate. A speaker should pay close attention to error factors before reporting a study in a speech.

How should one use these statistics in a speech?

1. The statistic must be meaningful to the listener. For this reason, large numbers should be rounded off without substantially distorting the results.

2. A speech should not contain so many statistics that the listener becomes confused.
3. Statistics are best used when they are applied to a situation that the listeners understand. That is, giving all of the numbers about how many suicides took place in the United States in a given year is not useful. Instead, if the listeners know that elderly people commit suicide more often than teenagers, the point is well made.

You might test yourself by checking the following statistics in an almanac or in the *Statistical Abstract of the United States:*

- Most people who are sentenced to die for a crime in the United States are African American males.
- Most people who commit suicide in the United States are teenagers.
- The state with the largest population in the United States is California.
- African American males are sentenced to death for a crime at a disproportional rate.

Testimony

Testimony is an account presented by one person. Were one to explain an account of the Battle of Gettysburg in the U.S. Civil War, he or she might use a letter written by a survivor to his wife. This would be a first person account of what happened. Another type of testimony is *expert testimony*. In most court cases, when there is an issue of the sanity of a defendant, both the prosecution and the defense present a psychologist or psychiatrist to testify about the sanity of the defendant. As you know, the experts usually present opposite views, and lawyers ask the jury to judge based on the credibility of the two experts.

The best types of expert testimony are those sources that appear unbiased or least biased. Assume that a speaker is discussing some experiments about a particular food or drug. One study shows that there are no side effects and the other illustrates that there are substantial side effects. The question might be *who* paid the researcher? If one study was undertaken by the pharmaceutical lab owned by the company that produced the drug and the other study was undertaken by the National Institutes of Health (NIH), the latter would probably be more credible. How many studies did tobacco companies undertake to illustrate that smoking cigarettes were harmless? How many did they publish?

In addition to expert testimony, the speaker may want to use a quotation from a layperson who has had a particular experience and has stated his or her views eloquently. Although such a view may have no validity from the standpoint of statistics, it may present a reasonable view of one person who illustrates how others may think or feel. A victim's thoughts of a crime; a low-level insider's view of the White House; and a person incorrectly convicted of a crime are all examples of people who may present views that the audience can identify with, yet who lack special expertise or prestige. The following example might be used to illustrate the state of customer service in America.

> I walked into the nearby grocery store, despite my often having felt that the service was terrible. I tried to choose the "best" line [the one on which I may get out the fastest]. For some reason, this never works. I was two people from buying my groceries when the checker put up a sign, "This line is closed." I graciously moved to the next line, now five people from the front. "Oops!" The scanner wasn't working. Two other checkers came over to try to help the one checker with the problem. Now there were seventeen people standing, awaiting one checker to do something about his scanner.

This is a situation in which many of the listeners probably have been involved, yet perhaps not in such an exaggerated fashion. The individual testimony is from a mere customer but one who has stated the views of many others.

Examples

In some cases, the speaker needs to use examples. More often than not, this information is not going to be found in the research gathering. The use of examples calls for creative thinking on the part of the speaker. If a speaker is explaining how to be a better movie critic, he or she may provide examples from various films to demonstrate effectiveness and lack of effectiveness from those films. The speaker may use *Titanic* and *Independence Day* to show the difference between films that have good and bad special effects. He or she may use *As Good as It Gets* and *Titanic* to demonstrate well-written and poorly written scripts. In this way, the speaker might explain how some films win Oscars and others do not, because of particular aspects of the films.

A speaker might use examples in a comparison and contrast pattern to show what happens to individuals over their lifetimes. To do this, the speaker might find examples from research or might create them. If the speaker creates an example, however, he or she should notify the audience that this is a hypothetical example. For example, this approach could be utilized in explaining how important it is to learn to read effectively while in high school. One example could be a person who never tried to read a textbook but depended on his ability to "fake it" in examinations. The other case could be a student who was always interested in reading. Although they both might attend college, the latter example is much more likely to find an easy-going four years.

Demonstrations

Demonstrations are sometimes entire speeches. At other times they are elements or supporting material for a speech. Especially in informative speeches, it is necessary to provide demonstrations. Demonstrations always provide an example through some action taken by the speaker. Audiovisual aids are more often used with demonstrations.

All of us are aware of various demonstrations. A chemistry teacher might demonstrate the particular effects when two chemicals are mixed together. Martha Stewart might demonstrate on television how to create decorations for the home. Bob Vila might demonstrate how to add a deck to your home. The purpose of a demonstration is to show how a skill or a device or a process or a procedure may be learned through knowledge.

Dale (1954) wrote that there are three ways of trying to explain something to the audience: telling, showing, and doing (see Figure 11.1). The least effective way of teaching people is by telling them about it. Showing (demonstrating) is much more effective. Finally, letting the other person do it is the most effective.

When most people have problems with some computer program, the last option that they feel is available to them is to read the instructions manual. This is partially because of laziness, but it is also because the book is merely telling them how to do it. The second option is to have someone show them how to do it. The best, though, is to have someone there while you do it yourself. Particularly if you do it several times while another watches, you would have learned how to use the program.

Demonstrations often require the use of visual aids. Demonstrations must be timed very accurately during a rehearsal for the speech, because they often take much longer than anticipated. Some potential uses of a

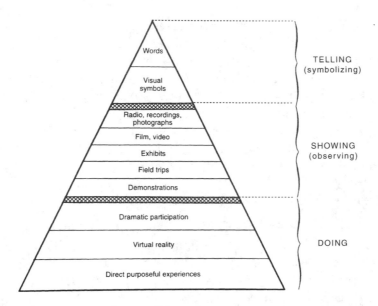

FIGURE 11.1   Cone of Experience

demonstration within a speech might be how to take your own blood pressure (for a speech on high blood pressure), how to read scanner labels (in a speech on saving money at the grocery store), how to find airfares on the computer (in a speech on saving money on travel).

If your instructor allows speeches that are strictly demonstration, the entire speech might be composed of how to select beef at the grocery store, how to make your own pasta, how to brew your own beer (in places where this is legal), or how to create your own Web site.

Narratives

Narratives are stories. They are typically longer than testimony. Sometimes they are taken from other sources, but most often they are created by the speaker. Narratives are often used in an introduction. They create a story that focuses the attention of the audience on the topic of the speech. Some speakers tell the beginning of the story in the introduction, saving the ending for the conclusion of the speech. Often speakers use narratives when introducing other speakers, especially stories about the speaker. The best narratives for a speaker to use are those of his own. By using one's own story, the speaker does not have to look at notes and will not forget the major points of the story.

Humor

When most of us think about humor, we think about jokes. As we all know, though, not everyone can tell a joke in a speech. Our experience has been that most speakers are not very good at it. There are several reasons: (1) The audience has already heard the joke before; (2) it may offend someone in the audience; (3) many speakers leave out important parts of the joke, including the punch line. For this reason, it is important to handle humor carefully.

The Transition from Research to Speech

It is fairly common for a student to find plenty of sources for a speech topic. However, the difficulty arises in trying to use the materials in a beneficial way. Perhaps the best way to think about this is to determine the main points and the materials that support the main points first. In a sense, then, you may think of each point as a minispeech. That is, how do you want to get this particular point across? We illustrate this idea with two different topics—one persuasive and one informative.

In the first instance, the persuasive speech, we are advocating a course in nonverbal communication at the university. Major point number one is to illustrate the importance of nonverbal communication on our lives. As the speaker reflects, the following notions become part of what may be part of the speech. A number of statistics state that the importance of nonverbal communication is that it accounts for between 65 and 93 percent of the emotional meaning of messages. The speaker also knows that while we take a number of courses (from English in elementary school through sophomore literature) in how to use words, most people never take a course in nonverbal communication. In addition, we know that we need to be aware of our nonverbal communication in a number of situations in life. Job interviews, speeches, and first meetings are good examples. We know that we can get a quotation from one of the professors who teaches nonverbal communication at the university. We might also interview a few students who have taken the course before.

Thus, we may have parts of a puzzle that look like Figure 11.2. We know that within the minispeech, we want to establish attention and the need to know. In addition, we must be concerned about the credibility of all of the information we have included in the speech.

In the second instance, in an informative speech about the causes of the U.S. Civil War, the speaker might find a substantial body of information about the topic. A narrative about the differences in the social life of Southerners and Northerners during the time might make a point. The speaker could find statistical information about the economy of the two sections of the country, including how they related to each another. The issue of slavery as a political issue may be a third cause. The purpose of the minispeech might be stated as "Although many believe that slavery was the sole cause of the Civil War, there are actually three interrelated causes." The speaker could use a visual aid to explain the relationships among slavery, social life, and economic life.

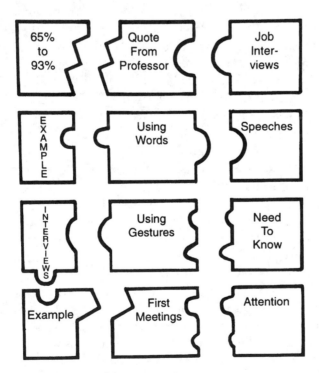

FIGURE 11.2   Fitting the Puzzle Together

Checking the Credibility of Sources

Now that we have substantial information that we can use in a variety of ways, we need to be even more concerned about the credibility of that information. We should check the information in a number of ways:

- Is the information biased? One-sided?
- Do the other sources agree with the information? If they contradict one another, you must either eliminate them or find a third source that supports one of them that you intend to use.
- Is the source up-to-date? How old is it?
- Does the source use reasoning that is legitimate?
- Does the source support conclusions with data, facts, information?
- Does the source separate fact from opinion?

SUMMARY

The effective speaker needs to balance the ways in which he or she uses the information that has been discovered. Facts and statistics are used as well as testimony and examples. Depending on the nature of the speech, the speaker may decide to use a demonstration. Narratives and humor may also be used to increase immediacy and the credibility of the speaker. Finally, the speaker should double-check all of the information in the speech to make certain that it is accurate, complete, and credible.

CHAPTER

12 Audio and Visual Aids

A wide variety of audio and visual aids may be used in a public talk. For example, one could use the chalkboard, an audiotape recorder, a videotape recorder, an object, a film, poster boards, flip charts, handouts, PowerPoint presentations, living animals, living people. The level of sophistication probably goes from writing on the board to PowerPoint presentations. In this chapter, we discuss the types of aids that have been and can be used, evaluate each, and develop some rules about using audio and visual aids when making a public talk. First, though, we discuss the reasons why a speaker should use or not use them.

The Purpose of Audio and Visual Aids

You should keep in mind that these are aids. Aids mean that the audio or visual helps to support what is being said in the talk. The visual aid should not be the focus of attention. Many people believe that using visual aids makes public presentation easier. Factually, though, this is often not the case. Most people who do not use audio and visual aids on a regular basis have difficulty with certain types of aids. How many times have you seen a presenter who did not know how to thread a film or switch on a videotape recorder, especially when using someone else's? Many teachers are laughed at because of their inability to use such simple machinery. Thus, before deciding on what kind of audio and visual aids to use, a speaker should decide whether to use them at all.

Some speakers think that using aids will increase the length of their speeches without adding to the information in the talk. This is not a good reason for using them. In these cases, speakers often use visuals as a backup for their outlines, with poster boards or flip charts used to indicate the major points of the speech. This use of visuals takes away from the talk itself, and the information is unnecessarily redundant of what the speaker is saying. Other speakers create exceptionally complex visuals in hopes of getting across a complex subject in a short amount of time. This rarely, if ever, works.

Why, then, should a speaker use a visual aid? In many cases, the answer is the same as why one would use a quotation. The answer is that the visual is the best way to get the point across to the listeners. Just as it is sometimes easier to draw a map to give someone directions, so, too, a visual might be worth a thousand words.

1. *Visuals help the listeners understand what is being said.*   For example, statistics are often best illustrated in a visual aid, especially when the numbers are large. Audience members have difficulty grasping such numbers without looking at them. Almost everybody has difficulty visualizing millions or billions or even hundreds of thousands. Let us suppose that you are delivering a speech that advocates the need to allocate more funding to alternative fuels for vehicles. We find that even with increased miles per gallon for newer vehicles, we are still using more gasoline than we did just a few years ago. From 1970 to 1992, the amount of gasoline used by vehicles in the United States (the world's largest culprit), increased from 92.3 billion gallons a year to 132.9 billion gallons per year. This is a 30 percent increase. Orally one might take the average number of gallons per vehicle to demonstrate that, in essence, one would have to purchase another tank of gasoline every three weeks to show the difference. In addition, we could show that while gasoline usage for cars has increased from 67.8 billion gallons to 73.9 billion gallons (an 8 percent increase), that for trucks has increased from 23.6 billion gallons to 58.0 billion gallons. This is a 58 percent increase. Thus, perhaps government should focus on alternative fuels for trucks.
Using a chart that shows

30% total increase
8% increase for cars
58% increase for trucks

helps to illustrate the point quite easily (*Statistical Abstract of the United States,* 1994). In this way, we avoid all of the figures of billions of gallons and focus only on the vehicles that are contributing most to the problem we are trying to solve. Another way of showing this pictorially is to show a truck as more than seven times the size of a car.

2. *Visuals help the listeners remember what they heard in the speech.*   Let us suppose you are advocating that the listeners become organ donors. You will find that the number of transplants for each of the following organs in 1960 was heart (62), liver (26), lung (0). By 1992, the numbers were heart (2,172), liver (2,954), and lung (401) (*Statistical Abstract of the United States,* 1994). This could be shown with a drawing of a heart comparing fewer than one hundred on a bar chart with twenty-one times that thirty-two years later. Drawings of the other organs could show a similar effect. With organs one needs to be careful not to offend the listeners with

detailed pictures. Good drawings probably serve you better for this purpose than do photographs, and in this case, black-and-white drawings
might be preferred.

3. *Visuals help gain and maintain the audience's attention.*   One should be
careful here, too, because the visual should not be a distraction from the
speech itself. For example, let us suppose you are giving a speech on a
magical potion for preventing stomach problems. The speaker can hold a
large paper bag with the potion in it and place it on a table in the front of
the room. This creates a curiosity on the part of those in the audience.
You could present information about the object throughout the speech,
finally taking an apple from the bag.

You should also recognize that there are visuals already available in
the room. If the speaker were discussing the misuse and abuse of electricity and the possibility of more brownouts and blackouts in the future as a
result, the speaker might just turn off the lights in the room briefly to
illustrate how important electricity is to us.

4. *Visuals may be used to illustrate the organization of the speech.*   This
may be the least important reason because the organization of the speech
should be obvious from the speech itself and by using signposts (notations
of "this is where we are"). However, one might use a visual such as a map
to illustrate the three major fronts that were taking place in World War II,
in Europe, in Asia, and in Africa.

5. *Visuals should help illustrate procedures or events.*   A chart might show
the steps in artificial resuscitation. A time line might demonstrate what
changes have taken place in the computer industry over the past twenty
years. But before any audio or visual aid is used in a speech, preparation is
necessary.

Preparation for Using Audio and Visual Aids

It is first and primarily important that a speaker *not* use any aid that may
be harmful or dangerous to the speaker or to members of the audience.
One of the authors' students presented a speech in which he was demonstrating the harmlessness of a balloon with hydrogen in it. The student lit
the string on the end of the balloon. The balloon floated to the ceiling
and created a mild explosion. Not only did the speaker lose all credibility,
but he also burned a hole in the ceiling and scared the rest of the class (and

the instructor) half to death. One should be especially careful about chemicals of any sort as well as any sort of weapons. Most weapons are illegal on college campuses anyway, but certainly they should not be used as visual aids in a speech class. Any illegal item is just as illegal in a speech class as it is anywhere else. Were one to speak on the medicinal effects of marijuana, it would not be advisable to use a plant as a visual aid (see Appendix A on ethics).

Second, the student should ensure that any and all visuals will work in the classroom in which the talk will be delivered. For example, are the electrical outlets in working order for a videotape, film, or overhead transparency presentation? Does the plug on the machine fit the outlet in the classroom? If one is using poster boards, will the boards stand on the place they are intended to stand? If they are to be taped to the board, will the tape hold throughout the speech? Are the visuals large enough to be seen by all members of the class? Thus, it is highly recommended that you practice the speech once with the visual aids in the room in which the speech will be delivered before you give the speech in class.

Using Specific Types of Audio and Visual Aids

As discussed earlier, many types of audio and visual aids can be used in a speech. These include, but are not limited to, chalkboards and marker boards; thirty-five-millimeter slides; film and videotape; audiotape; overhead transparencies; flip charts and posters; objects; models; and handouts. The first few of these are two-dimensional. The latter ones are three-dimensional. Each has advantages and limitations for the speaker; all considerations should be taken into account when choosing audiovisual aids.

Chalkboards and Marker Boards

The chalkboard is probably the most common visual aid used in a speech. In all probability, this is the type of visual aid most often used by your instructor. The reason is simple. The chalkboard is flexible; you can add and delete without much trouble. In addition, it is always there. However, when the chalkboard is used in a speech it appears that the speaker has been lazy in producing specific visuals for the speech and the speaker's credibility suffers. One good use for such a visual, though, is in explaining an idea visually when answering questions following the speech. This approach adds to the credibility of the speaker by utilizing what is available in a spontaneous way. One creative way to use the board is by using different colors of chalk for different aspects of your visual. It should be noted, though, that different colors of chalk are rarely available in the classroom; the speaker will have to purchase them and take them to the speech.

About twenty years ago, there was a popular art known as "chalk talk." This process involved exceptional drawings on the board using different colors of chalk. The method for making these drawings was to use an overhead projector with the drawings on them. Then the image was projected on the board. The student then traced the artwork on the board. This is extremely time-consuming, but it can be effective. You should check with your instructor, though, to determine whether to do this as it would have to be done before the class starts, and you would have to be the first speaker.

Marker boards avoid the problem of dust from the chalk, but they present additional problems. First, the speaker must make certain that he or she has the right kind and colors of markers available in the room. Second, when erasing marker boards, the erasure is often not as clear as a chalkboard. In addition, sometimes there are "bad spots" on the board on which one cannot write because of the accumulation of oil on the board.

Thirty-Five-Millimeter Slides

These slides are typically taken with a still camera. The slide projector must be a certain distance from the screen, which should be measured in practice. The speaker should also test the screen to make certain that he or she can roll the screen down and let it back up. Sometimes the handle is too high for the height of the speaker so that the speaker must ask for assistance. Generally, the speaker should be able to operate it independently in delivering the speech. Without practice, when the screen goes back up, it does so swiftly and with a great deal of noise. This is momentarily embarrassing.

The slides should be quite clear. A speaker may use slides that were taken by someone else or by the speaker him- or herself. The slides should be placed in order in the carousel. None of the slides should be upside down or sideways or backward. There should be no gaps between slides. It is best if the speaker has a remote control. Finally, the speaker should always have an extra bulb for the machine and should know how to replace it quickly and efficiently.

Film and Videotape

Historically, film has been used in support of speeches. However, this is rarely done today for a number of reasons. As we have discussed, films are relatively difficult to thread for the inexperienced user. In addition, film is not used as a primary medium today. Instead it has been replaced by the videotape. Any videotape should be viewed and edited in advance. Speakers should not use lengthy excerpts from videos. It is difficult to establish a rule about how long a video should be, but the video should probably comprise less than one-fourth of the presentation. If several excerpts are used, the video should be edited so that the speaker can easily go from one to the other without changing tapes. Inserts of black or blue background help the speaker know when to stop between segments.

The film or video should be clear, what video people call "air quality." The speaker should practice with the video to know where it begins and ends each time. The speaker must know how to turn on the television set and the video recorder as well as how to use start, stop, and pause Again remote controls are helpful. The speaker should also test the volume controls to make certain that the tape is neither too loud nor too soft to be heard. The tape should be removed at the conclusion of the talk in the event that the next speaker wants to use the machinery. If the next speaker does not wish to use it, the speaker should move the equipment before sitting down.

Audiotape

There are times when a speaker needs to use audiotape. To demonstrate bird sounds or regional vocal accents, the audio recording might work out well, unless the speaker can imitate the sounds. The tapes should be edited with limited use, just as with videotapes. The tape should be of exceptional quality and should be capable of being heard by everyone in the audience.

Overhead Transparencies

Overhead transparencies are easily made on computers these days. Drawings may be done with a paint software. For statistics, you can use Excel or a similar software program to make useful pie graphs, which show percentages of comparable data. These programs can also create other charts. It is important that the speaker select the right kind of transparency to use in the computer and printer. The size of print is also quite important. Eighteen (18) point type is probably the smallest size that can be seen by the audience. To print the overhead transparency, the speaker may take either of two actions. Some transparencies can be printed on the computer printer. If your printer does not have that capability, you may print the overheads onto paper and print the transparencies on a photocopy machine. Obviously, if you wish to have color overheads, you need a color printer or photocopier. Most copy stores have the capability of making color overheads, but they are relatively expensive.

Posters and Flip Charts

After the chalkboard, the poster is probably the second most commonly used visual aid in a speech. Problems that typically arise with posters are that students try to stand them on the chalk rack and they do not stand, there is a word misspelled on the poster, or the words are not easily seen in the back of the room. Any word in any visual should be spelled correctly, unless it involves a test of spelling. Audience members tend to focus on the misspelled words rather than the speech, and misspellings lower the credibility of the speaker. The poster should be clean, clear, and neat. If you have trouble lettering words on a poster, you should ask a friend for assistance. The poster needs to be checked out in practice to see whether it will stand or whether the tape will hold it up. When preparing, the speaker should also determine whether everyone in the class can see the poster. As already mentioned, another problem is that posters become overly complex, which complicates rather than simplifies the speech.

Flip charts have the same problems as posters. In addition, they have the problem that the speaker must turn them over periodically to get to the next visual. The speaker should always stand toward the audience, not the poster, flip chart, or other visual. The speaker needs to be facing the audience and should continue facing the audience while talking about the visual and when flipping the sheets.

Handouts

Another type of fairly common visual is the handout. Handouts should not be given to the audience members until after the speech is finished. The types of handouts that might be useful are those that indicate a Web site for further information or names, addresses, and phone numbers for additional information. If an organization deals with a problem, such as poor business practices, providing the local telephone number is acceptable. When a speaker wants the listeners to sign a petition, this should be done at the conclusion of the speech. The petition should already have some signatures, and the speaker should stand beside each audience member and hand the petition to each person individually, if your instructor allows time for this.

PowerPoint and Modern Technology

Virtually anything can be set up in a computer. Several different slides can be made, with or without print. Speakers can add drawings, photographs, charts, and the like. They can even have audio support. These Power-Point presentations, however, are quite difficult for the novice. Photographs will need to be scanned or a digital camera used. The equipment for the presentation includes a computer, a special overhead projector, and an LCD. Should you wish to use this technology, check with your instructor first.

No matter what type of audio or visual aid you use, you need to practice with it in the room in which you will make the presentation. The amount of time it takes to prepare visuals will vary, but a general rule is that it will take at least two hours for posters and several hours for videotapes and PowerPoint presentations. You should probably practice the talk in the room at least twice, which may take another hour or two.

Objects

Many speakers like to show actual three-dimensional objects when delivering their speeches. A speech on coin collections or stamp collections is an example. Many speakers pass the object through the class when speaking. This should *not* be done. If objects are passed around, it should be done either before the speaker begins or after the speaker has finished for at least two reasons: (1) The speaker may lose a coin or have a stamp damaged; (2) the audience members pay more attention to when they are going to hold the object than to listening to the speaker. Any object should be large enough to be seen by all in the room. The object should also be large enough so that the listeners can see whatever details the speaker is discussing. The speaker should stand the object up on a table or hold the object. However, the object should not be too large. One of the authors had a student present a speech on skydiving. The speaker brought a parachute into the class, through the class, and down the hall. Parachutes are big—probably too big for a speech in a classroom.

Models

Models might fall into three categories: objects, people, and animals. What we have already said about objects applies. A speaker might use a skeleton of a human being as a model. The size of a skeleton cannot be decreased or increased, so the speaker needs to practice with the skeleton to find out whether it works.

Even with practice, though, using other human beings or animals as models in a speech may cause difficulty. Animals are unlikely to behave in class as they do in practice. Humans, especially children, have similar problems. A person may get tickled or afraid. Volunteers should never be sought from the audience. One of the authors had a student deliver a speech on mouth-to-mouth resuscitation. The speaker (a male) had a female to help him demonstrate. As he began putting his mouth on hers, the audience members became more concerned about who the woman was than they were about how to help a person who has lost her breath. As it turns out, the victim was his wife, but the class did not know this until after the speech.

General Rules

The general rules are that you should use those audio and visual aids that support your talk. Visuals should be used to simplify what is being said. They need to be large enough for all to see clearly. Visuals should be kept out of the hands of the listeners. Use your hand nearer the visual when talking (laser pointers are not recommended). Visuals should be clean and neat, with all words spelled correctly. The visuals must help the listener conceptualize what you are saying. Plan for visuals increasing your time. Finally, visuals should be displayed only when using them.

SUMMARY

Audio and visual aids help support a talk. The speaker should keep this purpose in mind when using such aids. A visual should be "another way" of saying what is meant in the speech. Preparation time for visuals is somewhat lengthy. Certainly it takes longer to prepare a speech with visuals than a speech without visuals. The visuals should be checked and rechecked for accuracy and spelling. Visuals need to be made significantly in advance of the talk. The speaker should prepare for every element of the speech, including visuals in the room in which the speech will be delivered. Speakers must be courteous to other speakers and the instructor. When the use of the visual is complete, the speaker should take it with him or her unless the instructor says otherwise.

CHAPTER

13 Organizing Public Talk

Many remember those classes in which they are taught how to organize a term paper. Usually the teacher says, "Write your outline before you begin the paper." To some extent, this is like looking up a word in the dictionary that you do not know how to spell. How do you write an outline if you do not know what is going to be in the outline? This is a difficult process. As we have already learned, you must collect materials before you can organize the speech. Instead, we are recommending a "natural" way of organizing a speech. There are some pointers, though, that may tend to make a talk clearer and more persuasive.

A public talk or speech is not telling a few tales or jokes. That may be a comedy routine, but it is not a speech. Every public talk must have a purpose. There are two types of purposes in the preparation of a talk:

1. A *general purpose* is whether you intend primarily to inform or to persuade.
2. The *specific purpose* is the effect that you would like to have on your audience members as a result of your speech.

As an example, someone may deliver a speech to a local group. Her true purpose may be to gain clients for her law firm. That may be her purpose, but that is not the purpose of the speech. The specific purpose of her speech may be for the audience "to gain knowledge and insight about new copyright laws on the Internet." This statement of purpose is how it should be done. The specific purpose is written from the viewpoint of the audience. It states that the general purpose is to inform ("gain knowledge and insight") on the topic ("new copyright laws on the Internet"). At this stage, then, the speaker knows the topic and the specific purpose. The specific purpose should entail why audience members might want more knowledge about copyright law as it relates to cyberspace. The *why* is an indicator of what motivates audience members to listen to the speech. What kind of an audience might the speaker have if this is her specific purpose? To make this decision, we must know something about the audience. Which of the following groups would be a most likely audience for this speech?

- A civic club
- Other lawyers
- Students in high school
- Web masters (people responsible for Web sites)

As we consider the audience, we must first assess what they already know and what they need to know. A civic club (Lions, Kiwanis, Pilot, Civitan, etc.) would probably be too diverse to have much interest. That is, most of them do not know much about the topic, but they do not need to know or want to know much about it either. Strangely enough, most lawyers would also probably be too diverse. There are all types of lawyers just as there are all types of civic club members. Most students in high school neither have knowledge nor need to know. The only one of these four groups that might want to hear this speech is probably the Web masters. They have substantial knowledge of the Internet but know little about the law. In order to avoid violating copyright laws, they need to know about the law as it applies to their work. The basic rules of a specific purpose, then, are that the purpose is worded from the audience's perspective, that it indicates the specific purpose, that it includes the topic, and that it explains why the audience needs to know. Thus, the specific purpose of this speech, including the need to know, would be "for Web masters to gain more knowledge and insight about copyright laws on the Internet (to prevent being sued for violations)."

When one begins preparing for a speech, it is not necessary to create a title. This will be necessary to do so at some time, but not in the beginning. It should be noted, however, that sometimes a speech must be prepared weeks in advance because the organization sponsoring the speech will want to publicize the title.

Briefly we discuss some errors that students typically make in their statement of a specific purpose. First, the speaker states it from his or her perspective, not the audience's; for example: "to inform the audience about. . . ." Instead the speaker should conceive of the purpose from the viewpoint of the audience as in "to gain knowledge," "to learn the laws about," and so forth.

Organize and Support Major Points

Step 1: Write Down What You Already Know about the Topic

In a natural way of organizing, you should already know quite a bit about the topic or you would not be speaking on it. Reflect; think about what you know. What would you tell someone in a normal conversation about the topic? If there are any special key terms one may need to know, write them down. Assume that you will be talking with someone who initially knows nothing about the topic.

Let us assume that your topic is "how to use a word processing program." You would certainly want your audience members to understand what word processing is. Do not look for a dictionary definition; instead think about how you would describe a word processing program to someone else. If you have time in the speech to go into specific programs, you may want to define WordPerfect or Word. If you have only a brief time period, you may want to avoid too much confusion and simply talk about spacing, fonts, and editing. You must, however, begin at the beginning of what you already know. Write down everything you know.

Step 2: Develop Three to Five Major Areas That You Will Cover

The best way to do this is to take all of your computer printouts and/or all of the articles you have copied, and begin placing them in piles. The piles should each contain similar areas of word processing. One area might be about formatting. Anyone who has studied the format command in word processing will know that one might need to include fonts, paragraphs, tabs, borders, and columns under that command. Generally speaking, subtopics (or major areas) will fall into three to five areas. In most instances, you will not be allowed enough time to cover more than five subtopics.

Organizing an Informative Speech.   There are different patterns for organizing an informative speech and a persuasive speech. We will discuss each of these patterns in this chapter. We begin with organizing an informative speech by discussing chronological, spatial, cause–effect, problem–solution, and topical patterns.

Chronological Pattern.   The *chronological pattern* involves beginning with those elements that the audience already knows. This is referred to as the *principle of contiguity or proximity*. In a speech about "what to do in a medical emergency," you begin with the nature of the emergency. It might be helpful to define what an emergency is because 911 operators have indicated that many people call when there is no real emergency. Once you have defined an emergency, you may want to discuss different types of medical problems such as heart attacks, choking, and other physical injuries. Depending on how much time you have, you may want to limit your talk to one or two of these emergency situations. For example, if you have a younger class composed of people who have or are likely to have young children in the next few years, you may focus on choking. However, if the audience is composed of older individuals who may have their parents living with them, you may want to focus on heart attacks. Your organizational pattern should be a step-by-step approach. If you can think of an acronym for the steps, it helps the listeners remember what you have said. An *acronym* is a word formed by the first letter or letters of the major parts of a compound term. Of course, the first step in case of a medical emergency is to call 911. You may want to explain what information you should have handy in the event of such an emergency. For example, if you have baby-sitters, they may not know your address. The address, telephone number, and names of the parents should be near the telephone so that the sitter can easily call 911.

Spatial Pattern.   Some topics lend themselves to the spatial pattern. The *spatial pattern* indicates that the major points are organized by space or geography. For example, if you discuss the effects of *el Niño* on weather patterns of different parts of the country, you may want to use the spatial method. In a discussion of U.S. foreign policy, the arrangement of books in a library, designing your own house plans, making more efficient use of an apartment, or time management, you may want to use the spatial pattern.

Cause–Effect Pattern.   The *cause–effect pattern* of organization is used when you can state what happened and the results. Coaches may use this approach to explain why a team lost a game. However, they are more likely to use *effect–cause*. Both cause and effect, in either order, must be explained. For example, if you were discussing the environmental problems caused by the elimination of the rain forests, you could explain how cutting down trees causes such difficulties as there being less oxygen in the air. Another speech could be given on why the public schools need to obtain more and better computers so that the next generation will be better equipped to deal with the changing technological world. The cause would be the lack of satisfactory computers; the result would be a less educated and virtually computer-illiterate citizenry. The apathetic voting population would be the result (or effect) of recent political infighting between Democrats and Republicans at the national level. A case could be made for more judges and police officers to create a more efficient and effective judicial system. The cause might be that there are not enough public funds expended for judges and police officers; the effect—more crime and inefficient justice.

Problem–Solution Pattern.   Sometimes referred to as the need–plan method, the *problem–solution pattern* develops a difficulty first and later explains at least one manner in which the difficulty can be resolved. This pattern begins by explaining how the problem began. The problem should be explicitly defined. "How can we best deal with the problem of teenage cigarette smoking?" is a common concern in today's world. Many people want everyone to stop smoking, but teenagers are a special focus to stop the problem as early in life as possible. The problem is then investigated as to why it happens. For example, why do teenagers want to smoke cigarettes in the first place? Peer pressure, the romanticism of characters in television and movies, and imitating parents are likely reasons. What kinds of solutions have been used in the past? This step may discuss advertisements against smoking as well as increasing prices. The speaker would then explain why these solutions have not worked and suggest a new, innovative solution to the problem.

Topical Pattern.   The most widely used method of organization is the *topical pattern.* This is because many topics do not fall into the categories previously mentioned. An example might be a speech on different types of music. Jazz, blues, country and western, rock, and classical may be the categories or the terms to use for the major points of the speech. A speech on improving study habits might include time management, finding a suitable and regular place to study, finding tutors, and study teams. Although it is certainly possible to use another pattern of organization, these topics do not easily fall into a problem–solution, chronological, cause–effect, or spatial pattern.

Organizing a Persuasive Speech.   Although persuasive speeches might be delivered with some of the organizational patterns mentioned, specific patterns are used almost exclusively for persuasive speeches. These include the altruistic–ego pattern and Monroe's motivated sequence, although the problem–solution method might be used for either informative or persuasive speeches. The most utilized of these patterns is known as the *motivated sequence,* which was originally developed by Alan Monroe (1962) at Purdue University.

Monroe's Motivated Sequence.   The assumption of Monroe's pattern is that there is a certain progression in which people are motivated to change attitudes and/or behaviors. The first step in the system is the *attention step*. Here it is important to get the attention of the people in your audience. The second step is the *need step*. Here the speaker must ensure that the listeners have a reason to listen to the remainder of the speech. For example, a speech on developing your own retirement system through an individual retirement account (IRA) may not appear to apply to a need if your class is composed primarily of eighteen- and nineteen-year-olds. However, if the speaker begins with the statement, "You will need at least $2 million saved in order to meet the needs of your retirement," this sounds very challenging. Even a young person might want to know how he or she can raise that kind of money over the next forty-odd years. A speech on choking hazards of young children may not appeal to a group of childless students unless they know that most of them will have young children in the next five years. The need statement establishes a problem for those in the audience. The next step, *the satisfaction step*, provides a solution to the problem. Safety latches on cabinets in the kitchen and the bathroom might help prevent children's choking, for example. But Monroe was dissatisfied with these steps, which, in many ways, sound quite similar to the problem-solution method. He added a *visualization step*. In the visualization step, you draw a picture (with words) to show the listeners what might happen when an infant accidentally places a toy in his or her mouth and gets it stuck in the throat. You may use positive pictures about how this can be handled or prevented. You may provide negative examples of what could happen and the fear and potential disaster. You may provide a comparison and contrast to illustrate the differences between two sets of parents, one that takes your advice and the other that does not. Finally, the *action step* is a conclusion that explains to the audience what each member needs to do to bring about the purpose of the speech.

Altruistic–Ego Pattern.   Although this approach may sound ridiculous, it is based on the notion that people will do something not necessarily because they want to do so (although they do), but because they have good reasons to do so. Let us assume that you are speaking to motivate individuals to donate money to their alma mater. Most people want to do this anyway. However, a good motive is to help the institution to become even better than it was when they were there. There are also real reasons:

They get their names in the alumni newsletter; they get a tax deduction; they get a priority on purchasing football tickets.

This pattern has a six-step process. (1) The *introduction* is used to develop rapport and touch upon the issue. (2) In the *statement of social consciousness* the listener is told what a good thing he or she would be doing for the college and for higher education in general. (3) *The statement of selfish motives* provides the individual with motives that he or she is getting something out of it. (4) There is a restatement of *good reasons* (helping the institution). (5) There is a restatement of *real reasons* (football tickets). (6) In the conclusion the person is asked to donate the money (Richardson, 1967).

Step 3: Organize Each Pile

When preparing the talk, it is necessary to organize each subtopic. While format might be a subtopic of word processing, the speaker needs to decide how to talk about formatting. In the case of instructions, it is probably best to use an order from simple to complex (*the difficulty method*). Thus, the speaker needs to begin by defining each subtopic. Once the term has been defined, the speaker might want to identify where a computer user (an audience member) will find the format on a computer screen. After indicating where "format" is located and what it is, the speaker might need to explain what can be done with format.

Assuming that format includes fonts, paragraphs, tabs, and columns, the speaker will need to define each one and explain what each one does. The issue becomes how to order each of these units of the subtopic. Does it matter which comes first? In this case, it probably does not. With other topics, however, even the order of subsubtopics may be important. For example, chefs explaining how to prepare certain dishes must begin with the ingredients. Otherwise, the potential cook will find himself driving to the grocery store more often than preparing the dish. These instructional materials often follow a chronological order. The subtopics and subsubtopics must come first.

Step 4: Review Your Work

In reviewing one's order, several factors should be taken into consideration. In all probability, the speaker will find that he or she has some unneeded research materials. That is, there is some information that does not fit into a pile or is repetitive of other information in the pile. It should be thrown out! One of the major problems of most beginning writers and speakers is that they try to fit in everything that they have uncovered. Additionally, the speaker should ensure that there are not too many or too few subtopics. Two is probably too few. Six is probably too many. Because our goal is for the audience to recall what we have said, we do not want to make the task overly difficult. The number of subtopics between three and five depends on the audience's previous knowledge, the amount of time allotted for the talk, and the complexity of the topic.

Step 5: Order the Subtopics

At this point, the speaker should decide which pile comes first, second, and so on. Just as with the subsubtopics, the speaker must decide if there is any natural order—that is, does order really make any difference? If one is to use word processing, for example, the first thing the user needs to know is "How do I get some words on paper?" Therefore, one must open a new file. The chronological order may be good for the subtopics. One may need to decide whether to single space, double space, or triple space, as well as the size of type. The speaker must think through the process to determine what needs to come next. In this process, the speaker must act like a first-time computer purchaser. At this point, then, we have several subtopics in some order, and each subtopic has been organized.

Step 6: Establish Transitions from One Subtopic to Another

Transitions are words that connect one paragraph to another, or in our case, one subtopic to another.

There must be a method for showing the audience how each major point relates to the next one. If you were to take part in a conversation, you would probably ask questions if someone told you that a mutual acquaintance had committed suicide. Your thinking would probably go to why and how. Because questions are usually not allowed during the course of a speech, it is important to anticipate those places in the speech at which a question might be asked and to answer it at the appropriate time. One traditional means of doing this is through the use of signposts. *Signposts* are words or phrases that provide the listeners with a knowledge of where you are in the speech. A typical signpost is "I am going to discuss three types of . . . " Then you proceed to say, "The first type is . . . " "The second is . . . The last type is . . . " Although such an approach is better than no signposts at all, it certainly omits some significant and more appropriate methods. Some types of connectives or transitions may be to illustrate time (in chronological order) such as using the words *previously, in the future, during this time*. Others may include words or phrases related to making evident (*therefore*), returning to purpose (*to continue*), comparing (*in the same way*), opposing (*nevertheless*) (see Table 13.1). These connectives are far superior to no transitions at all or *next*. They make the speech sound more prepared and credible because the organization has been planned.

Using proper or suitable transitions makes a speech sound much better. Some of the phrases we have mentioned make the speaker sound as though he lacks the proper vocabulary. When contrasting two things, the speaker might use a transition such as *in contrast*. Instead of *finally* or *in conclusion*, a more appropriate term might be *therefore*. At this point, you have completed the body of the speech. Now is the time to begin developing the introduction and the conclusion.

Develop a Conclusion and Introduction

As we have already stated, one of the biggest problems that some people encounter is to try to develop the introduction first. The introduction and conclusion should be developed after the entire body of the speech (main points and subpoints) has been completed, along with the transitions. Although one might think that it is now time to develop the introduction, it may be easier to do the conclusion first. This is because you have just completed the last major point of the speech. You know where you began and where you have ended.

The Conclusion

A good rule of thumb for the overall organization of a speech is to tell the listeners what you are going to tell them (introduction), tell them (body), and then tell them what you have told them (conclusion). The conclusion of the speech should satisfy the requirement of tying loose ends, summarizing, and providing a solution to the problem. In addition, the conclusion should be where the speaker has his or her "last word." Just as in a court case, the lawyers' summations explain to the jurors how they would

TABLE 13.1   Types of Connectives

1. *Indicating time.*   previously, formerly, at the earlier period, anterior, contemporary, at the same moment, in the same period, throughout this period, during this time, meanwhile, in the meantime, upon this, by that time, already, now, since then, after this, thereafter, in the end, at last, at length, at a later time, henceforth, now that

2. *Making evident:*   thereof, thereby, thereto, therein, therefrom, in this case, in such a case, at such times, on such occasions, under these circumstances, in all this, in connection with this, here again

3. *Returning to purpose.*   to continue, to return, to report, to resume, along with . . . , as I have said, then, now, again, once more, at any rate, at all events

4. *Making reference.*   in point of, with respect to, as related to, concerning, as for

5. *Citing*   for instance, for example, to illustrate, by way of illustration, another case, a case in point is . . . , under this head

6. *Excepting.*   with this exception, this exception made, except for this, waiving this question, leaving this out of account . . . , excluded, exclusive of . . . , irrespective of . . . , excluding this point

7. *Summarizing.*   to sum up, to recapitulate, on the whole, briefly, in a word, in brief, in short, we have traced . . . , as we have seen, up to this point, yes, no

8. *Concluding.*   to conclude, finally, last, in conclusion, last of all

9. *Explaining.*   that is, to explain, in other words, this is as much to say, that amounts to saying

10. *Marking a change in tone or in point of view.*   at least, seriously, in all seriousness, jesting aside, to speak frankly, for my part, in another sense, as a matter of fact, in fact, to come to the point, in general, of course, you see, as the matter stands, as things are

11. *Comparing.*   parallel with . . . , allied to . . . , comparable to . . . , from another point of view, in the same category, in like manner, in the same way, similarly, likewise, a similar view, yet more important, of less importance, in contrast with, conversely

12. *Emphasizing.*   indeed, moreover, add to this, furthermore, besides, further, even without this, in addition to this, all the more, even more, into the bargain, especially, in particular, how much more, yet again, above all, best of all, most of all

(continued)

TABLE 13.1   Continued

13. *Judging.*   so, therefore, consequently, accordingly, thus, hence, then, in consequence, as a result, the result is, we conclude, because of this, for this reason, this being true, such being the case, under these circumstances, what follows

14. *Conceding.*   certainly, indeed, it is true, to be sure, it must be granted, I admit, true, granted, admitting the force of . . . , no doubt, doubtless

15. *Opposing.*   yet, still, nevertheless, however, on the other hand, at the same time, nonetheless, only, even so, in spite of this, the fact is . . . , after all

16. *Refuting.*   otherwise, else, were this not so, on no other supposition, on the contrary, no never, hardly

Source: E. Brenneke Jr., & D. L. Clark (1930), *Magazine article writing* (New York: Macmillan), pp. 139–142.

like the jurors to vote, the speaker tells the listeners what he or she wants them to do, how to feel, what to know. At a bare minimum the conclusion should summarize the body of the speech. The conclusion might end with a quotation, an illustration, a challenge, or humor. Here you should also remind listeners of your need statement in the introduction.

The Introduction

The introduction should begin with an attention getter. This may be a quotation or a story, especially a personal story, because you want the listeners to know how you became interested in the topic. For example:

> It was the ides of March in the South. The television weatherman was always talking about crises. There might be a thunderstorm or a tornado. There might be rain. It was the middle of March. The day before the weather was beautiful, about 75 degrees. But on this day, the weather people all over town were saying that there was going to be snow.
>
> I drove home early that day, and on the way I observed tons of people going to the grocery store to purchase items for the big incoming "snowstorm." Yeah, right.
>
> I finally got home. Later that afternoon, a little snow started to fall, but this was the middle of March, in Birmingham, Alabama. There wouldn't be

much snow. By night's end there were several feet of snow on the ground. Suddenly, the electricity was off. Of course, I had a heater, but the gas heater had an electrical blower. I had a fireplace, but I had no wood. That was the first time that I began my belief in gas logs for the fireplace.

This introduction makes the speaker the victim, a rather stubborn and somewhat unintelligent victim, but a victim. It also provides a way for the audience to identify with the speaker. The speaker has created a problem and a solution in the introduction. In all probability, there will not be many surprises. The speech will be about gas heating, or it could be about generators, or about not being stubborn, or about how meteorologists determine their forecasts. In any case, though, the speaker has drawn the attention of the audience.

An introduction may begin with a statistic or several statistics. It may begin with a rhetorical question. It should first attract attention, and then explain to the audience members why they need to know about the information in the speech. It should establish rapport between the audience and the speaker. The "he's just one of us" notion that many politicians try to create should be created by the speaker. Following attention, need, and rapport, the speaker should develop a *preview* of what will be in the speech (tell them what you are going to tell them). The exception to this is when you do not want the audience to know the ending until the end.

Transitions

The final steps are to develop transitions between the introduction and the body of the speech as well as between the body and the conclusion. You will find that your conclusion is most effective if you bring it back to the introduction. As example may be used as in the preceding case:

> So today, I pay more attention to the weather. I know that the majority *may* be right. I have gas logs in my fireplace. I no longer worry about freezing to death in a snowstorm. The next time you see bad weather, think gas.

Now we have organized the entire speech. These, however, are technical or structural organizations. It remains necessary to determine how to present different kinds of information, which we discuss in the next chapter. But going back to the instructor asking us to develop an outline, how do we do it now that we are finished? And why do it now?

Developing an Outline

There are two types of outlines. A formal outline is much like a detailed table of contents. A working outline is the notes you will use in your speech.

The Formal Outline

Your instructor may want you to turn in a *formal outline*. A formal outline is what you remember from English classes. The main points are listed with Roman numerals. The subpoints are illustrated with capital letters, A, B, C. Your support for each of the subpoints is shown with Arabic numbers, 1, 2, 3. Some speakers formulate their outlines in even more detail. As an example, let us compose a rather simple outline on delivering effective speeches.

Delivering Effective Speeches

   I. Introduction (Pile I)
      A. Attention statement
      B. Need statement
      C. Statement of rapport, 1
      D. Statement of rapport, 2
      E. Preview

  II. Gathering Materials
      A. Where to go (Pile IIA)
         1. Library (Visual Aid 1)
         2. Internet (Visual Aid 2)
      B. Recording materials (Pile IIB)
         1. Source cards (Visual Aid 3)
         2. Information cards (Visual Aid 4)

 III. Organizing Materials
      A. Developing major points (Pile IIIA)
         1. Three to five
         2. Around the same subtopic
         3. Discarding useless information
      B. Developing subpoints (Pile IIIB)
         1. Three to five
         2. Two or more sources

IV. Adding Visual Aids
   A. Two-dimensional aids
   B. Three-dimensional aids

V. Practicing the Speech

VI. Delivering the Speech

VII. Conclusion

The Working Outline

The *working outline* is the outline that the speaker uses to deliver his speech. Such an outline may be less specific and detailed than the formal outline. This outline is used to keep the speaker abreast of where he or she is during the speech. Quotations should be printed word-for word or the source of the quote should be used. The same is true for statistics. Any specific detail that the speaker wants to cover should be on this outline. It is best that such an outline be on a series of 4- by 6-inch note cards or notes that are easily used. Here is an example of such a card:

```
1                                                       1
IIA. Going to the Library
■ Access through the Internet at home
■ Access through the library's computer system
■ Using indexes (Visual aid 1)
  Word selection for topic
  Using synonyms
  Using the most updated information
■ Avoiding books
```

Note that the card number is placed in both corners of the top of the card. This prevents the speaker from fumbling around with the cards. The number should also be written on the back of the card. The working outline should be written on only one side of the card.

SUMMARY

Once the speaker has done the research, it is important to begin placing the information in some order for the speech. Materials should be placed along major topic areas. After this step has been completed, the speaker should organize the information within major topics (or piles). The conclusion and introduction should not be considered until the body has been completed. Unnecessary, redundant, or nontopical information should be deleted from consideration. Next the speaker needs to develop a working outline of the speech. At this point, though, there may be a problem with too many statistics, too many stories, or the like. The next chapter considers a balance of types of information to make the speech more appealing to the listeners.

EXERCISE

This section contains twelve parts of a speech outline using Monroe's motivated sequence. These parts are not in order. Decide the order in which they should go. You may want to tear out the pages and cut the pages in half to undertake this task. After you put them in order, indicate for what step of the sequence (attention, need, satisfaction, visualization, or action) each sentence is being used.

_____ A   Although taking away all of the guns may sound like a good idea, it is probably impossible.

_____ B   My friend, Ryan, came home last week. When he opened his front door, he found his fourteen-year-old daughter on the floor. She was dead.

_____ C   There are many ways to die: natural causes, accidents, suicide, murder. Unfortunately, murder is too often the case for fourteen-year-olds.

_____ D   Imagine your own child or the child of a friend.

_____ E   In 1992, 68 percent of murders were committed with a gun.

_____ F   Write your congressperson suggesting that all handguns be test-fired and recorded. I am providing you the address so that you can do so _today_. The life you save may be your child's.

_____ G   Some measures have been taken by the federal government. Some states, too, have even stricter laws. Yet they are not sufficient.

_____ H   But the Second Amendment was created long ago; today's technology provides a means for keeping track of the location of guns, without interfering with legal possession.

_____ I   With this technology, each handgun can be fired once and a picture of the bullet placed in a computer file, along with registration of the serial number. We always know who is responsible.

_____ J   Your child or your friend's child goes to play with another little friend, and they play with the father's handgun.

_____ K   Some groups, especially the National Rifle Association (NRA) and gun manufacturers, want to prevent *any* kind of restriction with their Second Amendment arguments. They want to avoid liability. But some states are already creating liability for guns, just as they do with automobiles.

_____ L   Using the computer system, owners would become more responsible, keeping track of their guns, locking them up, reporting thefts, and so forth

CHAPTER

14   The Big Four

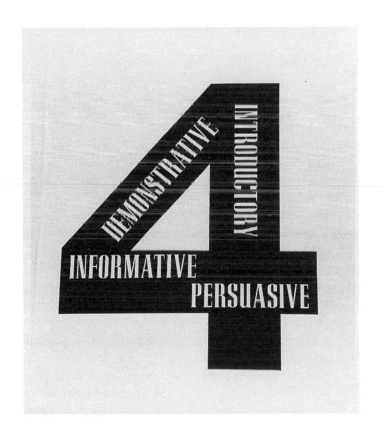

The previous chapters in this text have been devoted to the reasons for public talk, the basics of public speaking, the fear and management of public talk, the speaker's image, audience analysis, listening, presentational skills, nonverbal and verbal effectiveness skills, gathering materials, and organization. This chapter reviews the four major types of presentations you are likely to encounter in either the classroom or public life. These big four are

1. A speech to introduce another person
2. A speech to inform or brief others about an idea or concept
3. A speech to influence or persuade others to believe something or do some act
4. A speech to demonstrate a concept or idea

The Introductory Speech

"The speech of introduction is usually designed to introduce another speaker or to introduce a general topic area and a series of speakers" (DeVito, 1997, p. 407). The main purpose of a speech of introduction is to gain the attention of the audience and effectively and efficiently keep the audience's attention while you introduce a person or an idea. This section focuses on the introduction of another person because many times in the future you will be asked to introduce either formally or informally your peers, coworkers, supervisors, or guests to audiences of either one or many persons at various social and organizational functions.

Although the introductory speech is also informative, it is usually not as long as a formal informative presentation. An introductory speech may be as lengthy as three minutes or as brief as one minute. Remember, you are introducing another person or persons, and your goal is to raise interest and keep the audience's attention. You never want the introduction presentation to go too long or you may lose your audience.

For this presentation and the informative, persuasive, and demonstration speech, keep in mind the following formula:

Goal or Purpose + Audience Analysis + Organization
+ Effective Delivery = Effective Speech

Several guidelines to use for the introductory speech follow:

- Your goal is to get the audience's attention and interest. You need to make the audience want to listen to the speaker you are introducing.
- You must be able to answer the question "Why should people listen to this person?"
- You need to establish the speaker's credibility without doing overkill.
- You need to be brief and yet comprehensive.
- You should never review the speaker's topic. Let the speaker cover his or her topic.
- Never say, "This person needs no introduction." Often not everyone in an audience knows the person you are introducing, and it is rude to the speaker not to tout some of his or her accomplishments.

The Informative Speech or Briefing

Informative messages are messages that are "directly intended to influence understanding and are not specifically designed to influence attitudes in a predetermined manner" (McCroskey, 1997, p. 166). The goal of the informative presentation is to inform, instruct, educate, brief, and explain concepts or ideas to an audience; it is not to persuade. The following guidelines should be used when developing a speech to inform or brief an audience about a concept or idea.

- Have a credible, reliable speaker sending the message. Therefore, you must be viewed as a credible, reliable source of information before you can inform someone.
- Remember that the two primary characteristics of informative messages are clarity and objectivity (McCroskey, 1997, p. 171). Therefore, you must be clear, honest, articulate, and nonbiased in your presentation. If you appear to be ambiguous, dishonest, inarticulate, or biased about the information you are imparting then your audience may not listen or they may perceive you as trying to influence them.
- Use analogies, factual examples, hypothetical examples, statistics, data, and even visual aids when attempting to inform or brief an audience about an issue or concept.

- Be able to answer the question "Why would my audience want to hear this?"
- Be able to answer the question "Should I give all the information at this time or should I leave some information for the next informative presentation?"
- Remember that the purpose of the informative presentation is to raise the knowledge and understanding level of an audience. Often companies explain benefits to employees in an informative presentation. Often the president of the United States explains or informs the public of his intentions.

Informative speeches can range in time from five to seven minutes up to an hour. It depends on the situation, audience, information, and speaker. Lobbyists often can speak up to an hour informing others about their ideas.

The Persuasive Speech

According to McCroskey (1997) some "messages are directly intended to influence attitude and are specifically designed to influence understanding and are designed unconsciously to influence attitudes" (p. 166). These are the persuasive messages. Several factors you should consider in preparing your persuasive speech follow:

- Keep in mind that preparing a speech to persuade others to change attitudes or behavior is not easy. Often you are confronting a hostile audience. Chances are you cannot change some hostile audience's attitudes or behaviors, but perhaps you can make the audience think about change. You are most likely to change an undecided, disinterested, or uninformed audience's attitudes and behaviors. For example, speaking to the NRA about the dangers of guns and gun control will not be a pleasant experience. Now, if you are in favor of guns and less gun control, then you are speaking to the already convinced. When an audience is already convinced, it is an easy presentation because you are "preaching to the choir."
- You must be a credible, trustworthy source or your audience will reject your ideas immediately.
- Remember the goal of a persuasive presentation is to influence or change a person's attitudes or behaviors. Therefore, all speech effort is directed toward this goal.

- As in informative presentations, you should use statistics, data, factual examples, hypothetical examples, analogies, visual aids, and arguments to make your case. Often you need to present all sides of an issue, then clearly show support for your side of the issue. For example, when speaking about using condoms for safer sex, you should discuss why people do not choose to use condoms, then review the safer sex issue. This assures the audience that you are well educated about the use of condoms in sexual relations.

- You can also use rational and emotional appeals during a persuasive presentation. For example, Mothers Against Drunk Driving (MADD) uses both types of appeals when talking with various groups about drinking and driving.

- You must be able to answer the following questions: "What is the importance of my topic? Why should I talk about this subject? What examples or arguments can I present that support my ideas? Why should people support my ideas, attitudes?" Finally, be able to answer the so what question "So what does this information mean to the audience?"—and, "What should the audience do?"

Persuasive speeches can range in time from five to seven minutes up to an hour. In the U.S. Senate, senators will speak for as long as an hour when attempting to get other senators to support their ideas.

The Demonstration Speech

According to DeVito (1997) in using demonstration (or in a speech devoted entirely to demonstration), you would explain how to do something or how something operates (p. 333). Often in giving a demonstration speech you actually demonstrate or show how the idea, innovation, or object works. For example, you might demonstrate how to give CPR using a lifelike medical figure. You might demonstrate the basics of speech making by giving a simple, short presentation. You might demonstrate how to change the oil in your car by doing so. In short, a demonstration presentation is an informative demonstration about how something works. Here are some key ideas about how to present a demonstration speech:

- When planning a demonstration speech, outline the actual information you plan to use in the demonstration in an orderly, sequential manner. Have another person go through the sequence with you.

Perhaps this observer can spot nonsequential steps or flaws in your demonstration.

- You need to keep the demonstration part of the presentation short and sweet. If a demonstration drones on too long, the audience will become bored and lose attention. For example, in many computer training workshops the demonstrations are too long, tedious, and overly complicated so the audience's attention decreases rapidly. Do not use too many visuals, materials, or steps. When the demonstration becomes confusing, it is over. For good examples of demonstration speeches, watch some of the more successful infomercials on television.

- Again, use materials to support your demonstration, but do not let materials, handouts, and visuals speak for you.

- If possible make sure your audience can participate in the demonstration aspects of the speech. You will need to make some of these preparations in advance, especially if you intend to use an audience member as a volunteer.

- Encourage but control the questions from your audience. Encourage audience members to ask some questions while you go through the demonstration but keep verbose talkers from interrupting the flow of your presentation.

- If at all possible, make the demonstration presentation not only informative but also fun.

Keep in mind that demonstration speeches may be longer than the average informative or persuasive presentation. Demonstration speeches may require ten minutes to an hour or more. Their length depends on the audience, topic, situation, and time allowance.

SUMMARY

This chapter reviews the four primary speeches you are likely to give in the future. These presentations are the introductory speech, the informative speech, the persuasive presentation, and the demonstration presentation. With the guidelines and examples in this chapter, and the guidelines in this text, you should be prepared to manage the big four.

APPENDIX A

The Ethics of Going Public

Although many people discuss the concept of ethics, what they mean by ethics varies from individual to individual. There is general agreement that a speaker should not plagiarize the work of someone else, for example. Sometimes, though, we confuse what is legal, what is ethical, and what is bad taste or bad form. For this reason, we briefly discuss each of these because all are important when sharing information publicly.

Legality

Something is *illegal* when it violates the law of a city, a state, or a country. In the United States there are few laws about what someone says in public because of the First Amendment to the Constitution. This amendment reads:

> Congress shall make no law respecting an establishment of religion, or prohibiting the free exercise thereof; or abridging the freedom of speech, or of the press; or the right of the people peaceably to assemble; and to petition the Government for a redress of grievance.

Within those few words are encapsulated freedom of religion, speech, the press, assembly, and the redress of grievances. Here we are discussing only the freedom of speech.

Most of us have heard that you cannot yell "fire" in a movie theater unless there is a fire. Well, of course, you could. However, the fact is that you could be prosecuted for doing so because such an action endangers public safety. If someone were hurt or killed as a result of your action, you could also be sued in court, with the likely consequences that you would lose the case.

Several colleges and universities have created certain "rules" on their campuses over the past ten years that say students cannot use certain racial or sexist terms. In some cases, these rules are upheld as a right of the institution and in other cases they are found to be in violation of the First Amendment. A significant factor appears to be whether the college is public or private. The legal issue, though, would be whether the institution receives federal funding, and most of them do. Even so, private schools have more leeway to establish such rules. Public institutions, because they are arms of the state, are generally not allowed to make such restrictions. Over the years, in large measure because of the Fourteenth

Amendment, states are required to follow the same constitutional guidelines as is the federal government (Congress).

What are the legal restrictions on giving a speech?

1. *You cannot publicly state certain kinds of information.*   For example, the Securities and Exchange Commission (SEC) restricts what is called insider trading. Thus, if you were a stockbroker who got some information from a friend that American Telephone and Telegraph (AT&T) was about to acquire a major share of Microsoft, you could not provide that information to a group of people interested in buying stocks. In this situation, you would not be allowed to disclose such information privately either.

2. *You are not allowed to publicly state illegally obtained information.*   If you broke into the offices of Microsoft and discovered information about a merger with AT&T, you could also be in trouble. In this case, you would not be prosecuted for stating the information so much as for how you obtained it. In a sense, information is a commodity that can be stolen similarly to a television set or a pair of shoes. There are also laws about what information you can take from work. For example, if you worked for Microsoft and quit your job, should you give a speech about some "secrets" of the Microsoft Company, you could be sued and would probably lose the case. The information that you receive at work as well as the information you create at work belongs to the organization for which you work. A *copyright violation* is when you publish information that belongs to someone else. Although one cannot copyright an idea, such as public speaking, a person can copyright the combination of words used in his or her work. When using a quotation, for example, in a publication, you should state the source of the information. (The ethical equivalent is plagiarism, which is discussed later.)

3. *You are not allowed to disclose governmental classified information.* Should you have information about where Central Intelligence Agency (CIA) operatives are living and working, you should not state this information to others. First, it may have been, and probably was, illegally obtained; and second, classified information belongs to the government and those whom the government allows to have and use it.

4. *You are not allowed to state opinions or facts that incite a riot.*   This is similar to the yelling fire example. When your words are determined to cause a group of people to participate in illegal activities against other people or the government, you may be guilty of inciting a riot.

5. *You are not allowed to defame the character of another person.*   Referring to another person as a "thief," a "traitor," or a "cheat" is referred to as libelous *per se*. In addition, you cannot say things about a person that you know are untrue based on other facts you possess. Although there are some exceptions to this rule (e.g., using a statement in a comedy routine or writing a movie review), it is best if we consider it across the board. Certainly you can disagree with someone else's ideas, but it is best to do so without referring to the person's character (referred to as an *ad hominem* argument).

These, then, are basic rules about the law of presenting information publicly. Most will never be an issue in the classroom. What some teachers do, though, is to require that certain subjects may not be used for a speech or that certain words may not be used in a speech. For example, let us suppose that you advocate the growing of illegal marijuana plants in your dormitory room. What if the teacher said that you cannot advocate anything illegal? You would not have violated a federal or state law by advocating growing the plants. Did the teacher restrain your First Amendment rights? Probably not. What the teacher did was to provide you with some guidelines for what may constitute responsible speech. *Legal speech and responsible speech are not the same.* What if the teacher failed you because of your delivering the speech on growing marijuana plants? Do you have a legal recourse? Probably not. Again, the teacher graded your speech on the basis of how responsible the speech was. Thus, speech topics such as how to cheat on your income taxes without getting caught, how to grow marijuana plants, and how to cheat on a test all fall into the category of irresponsible speech. Why are these topics irresponsible? Because you are not following one of the basic principles of going public as set out by Aristotle some 2,400 years ago.

The Concept of Goodwill

Aristotle wrote that the speaker must have goodwill as part of his credibility. Goodwill refers to the *intentions* of the speaker. Suppose a candidate for public office were to state that if elected he or she would provide more services from government and drastically cut taxes at the same time. Of course, the candidate is stating something that is unreasonable. Most of us would agree that this is what many candidates do. There is nothing illegal about telling a lie when running for office; otherwise, we would have few elected officials outside of the jail cells. It is, however, not responsible speech.

Should a speaker advocate that the audience shoplift, the consequences could be grave when a member of the audience took the speech seriously. Although advocating an illegal activity is not illegal *per se*, it is possible that you could be arrested for conspiracy. Most people in a speech class are unlikely to advocate illegal activity. A speech that favors legalizing marijuana falls into a different category than does a speech about how to grow marijuana without getting caught. A speech on legalizing marijuana is simply an issue of policy. The topic has been used many times by students in public speaking classes across the country over at least the last fifty years. The argument usually goes something like this: We would have less crime if marijuana were legalized. Marijuana is not as dangerous as cigarettes. Were marijuana sales legal, they could be taxed as another source of income for the government. The topic is not an especially good one because it is so trite that most teachers have heard it dozens of times. Of course we would have less crime, because one crime had been eliminated as a crime. If we legalized everything, we would have no crime. The issue regarding a comparison with cigarettes is a shaky one because we are more in the process of making cigarettes illegal than we are in making marijuana legal. Finally, by taxing marijuana there is the possibility that more sales would be made illegally to avoid the tax. Thus, this topic is not illegal or not especially unethical, but practically it is not a good topic. Finally, the question must still be asked: "How does legalizing marijuana benefit the members of the audience?"

Let us suppose that the speaker chooses the topic of comparative shopping. In this talk, the speaker provides information about buying some items in volume, the use of coupons, and the concept of lower prices on some items during certain times of the year. Assuming that the speaker has no connection with the stores and does not advocate a particular store, this topic sounds as though it would include the notion of goodwill toward the audience. It is sometimes easier to justify goodwill in an informative speech than in a persuasive speech. This is because the goodwill of the speaker comes into question more often when it appears that he or she has something to gain by getting the audience to take some action.

Suppose the speaker discusses how to save money by buying some goods by not going to a store. Obviously there are several different possibilities for this speech. The speaker could talk about buying some products over the Internet or could discuss catalog shopping. But let us suppose that the speaker focuses on personal care products such as skin creams and the like. He or she presents Avon as a likely candidate. In the process of the speech (or afterward), the audience discovers that the speaker is an Avon salesperson. Although the topic itself could have held a goodwill tendency toward the audience, the speaker has crushed that goodwill by bringing the audience back to something that would benefit *the speaker* more so than them. The speaker should try to resist selfish intent.

The Ethics of Public Speaking

1. *The speaker should ensure that the material in the speech is his or her own.* Obviously if the speaker does library research, some or all of the material comes from somewhere else. However, it is most important that the speech not come from a file owned by some group. The speech should not be a condensed version of another speech. In fact, the speech should not be composed of material from only one source. It is the responsibility of the speaker to find several different sources and to provide references in certain places.

A *reference* in a speech is somewhat like a footnote in a paper. Anytime a quotation is used, the speaker should state its source. For example, "As John Kennedy said in his Inaugural Address, 'Ask not what your country can do for you—ask what you can do for your country.' " It is not necessary to provide a full bibliographical reference in a speech. You do not have to provide the author's name, title, journal name, volume, and page number. You should note the important features of the reference, however. For example, you want to provide the author's name. If the author is not easily recognized by the audience, you may want to say that "she is a professor of mechanical engineering at the Massachusetts Institute of Technology." By providing this information about your source, you are undertaking ethical behavior and adding credibility to your own speech. You should not refer to another source unless you found it and read it.

For example, let us suppose that you found a journal article in which another journal article is quoted and footnoted. You should not simply use the quote and the name of the cited author in the footnote, because sometimes there are errors made in journal articles, and you do not want to be caught providing the same wrong information. It is best to look directly at the article cited in the secondary article. Aside from quotations, most often you should provide the source for statistics, especially if the statistics are usually not to be believed by the audience. You might say, "According to the Securities and Exchange Commission (SEC), in 1995, there were . . . " Anytime you take some information from a source with such specific information, you should include the source of the information. Finally, if you use information that may be unusual or unbelievable to the audience, you should state its source. It is good to provide the author and the date even if you do not state the publisher, place of publication, or edition. Information taken from the Internet is especially suspicious. Often sources are omitted. Take care to ensure that you know where your information was derived and provide that information to the audience.

A student asked one of the authors of this text whether plagiarism is illegal. The fact is that it is not. If it is a copyright violation, then it is illegal. Otherwise, it is plain plagiarism. The student asked, then, what is wrong with it? What is wrong with it is that it violates a most sacred possession. Plagiarism is the theft of someone's ideas. Instructors will provide major sanctions for stealing someone else's work whether it is from *Reader's Digest* or another student's file.

2. *The speaker should abide by a privacy agreement that was requested by a source.* Let us suppose that you are delivering a speech about insider trading. You have interviewed a person who works for a major financial firm. He tells you that he knows of several cases in which insider trading has taken place, but he does not want to be used as a source. Otherwise, he might get into trouble himself. You may say: "According to one of my interviews with an employee of a major financial firm. . . ."

3. *The speaker should provide complete information.* A major network radio commentator once provided an editorial about how much liquor is consumed in Washington, DC, each year. He derived his statistics this way: He took the amount of liquor sold in DC. He divided that by the city's adult population. This is a distortion of information. He knew better.

The audience may not. But consider the following facts. There are a substantial number of hotels in Washington, DC, that purchase liquor. Government agencies purchase liquor. Finally, government and other workers who live in nearby Virginia and Maryland purchase liquor in DC because it is less expensive due to the lower taxes. A great deal of liquor is purchased in DC, but all of it is not drunk by people who live in DC. Even though a piece of information may be against the point that you are trying to make, you should ensure that you are providing a full report of the information that you have.

Choices in Etiquette

We have discussed what is legal and what is ethically right. We now turn to the issues that are of concern in etiquette or manners. For example, in most places the concept of politically correct language is a matter of etiquette. *Politically correct language* is the use of terms that do not offend others. Racial epithets, sexist jokes, and ethnic gags all fall into the category of politically incorrect language. As a speaker you should be especially concerned about the possibility of offending people. Even if we forget the kinds of examples just stated, a speaker who talks about large people or aliens might offend someone in the class. We should remember that these concerns are not legal or ethical concerns on most campuses, but they are concerns in the realm of etiquette. Other types of language may sound offensive to listeners. Obscenity and profanity are generally composed of words that should not be used when speaking in public. The reason is that these words might offend one or more members of the audience, and your speech may not be taken seriously and certainly will not be effective.

Respect for the Audience

The speaker should be concerned at all times about respect for the listeners. Not only may certain words be offensive, but also certain topics and perspectives may be offensive. Although a speech in favor of maintaining legalized abortion might be an acceptable topic, the speaker should recognize that not all members of the audience will have the same view. Topics that derogate one particular religion should be avoided. Statements that derogate certain people in the class, or people within certain classes, should also be avoided. Derogating statements about overweight people, anorexic people, short people, older people, and the like should be avoided; as well as statements about one's sex, sexual orientation, ethnic group, socioeconomic class or background, or region of the country. In short, the speaker should be concerned about his or her respect for the audience in general and each member of the audience in particular.

Although a speaker may advocate a certain position, he or she should realize that intelligent people may have an opposite opinion. The more controversial a topic, the more likely this is the case. In arguing against another perspective, the speaker should take care to provide evidence from objective sources and to use the arguments of credibility and logic to sustain his or her views. A speaker who believes that the audience may be composed of a substantial number of people who disagree should use a two-sided argument, respecting although not agreeing with the other point of view. The speaker should assume intelligence on the part of those who may disagree.

Respect for the Speaker

There are also responsibilities on the part of the listeners. As a listener, you should actively listen to what the speaker is saying. If you disagree, take notes so that you may ask questions at the conclusion of the speech. You should be courteous. You should not enter the room nor create any interruptions while a speaker is talking. You should not evaluate the speaker's performance on anything other than what he or she has said in the talk.

General Ethics and Etiquette

The general rule is that you should treat the other as you would wish to be treated. If you are the speaker, respect the listeners. If you are a listener, respect the speaker. As a speaker you should be honest, open, and abide by the rule that the best arguments are those that utilize the principles that have been outlined for speaking over the past two thousand years. The speaker should be honest. This means that there should be no conscious distortions of information. The speaker should be open. The speaker should be accepting of the possibility that other options may improve upon his own ideas. Finally, speakers and listeners should be aware that arguments are not heated conflicts but are civilized debates using credibility, logic, and emotion in a manner to persuade (Tannen, 1998). Evidence can be questioned for its validity. Arguments may be dismantled to illustrate their fallacies. In the end, no one may have his or her mind changed, but the search for better ideas will improve the knowledge and wisdom of all parties.

A Note on Objectivity

One of the most important features of the ethical speaker is that he or she attempts to avoid blatant bias. Many would say that every source is biased, and that may be true. However, there are methods for determining the degree of bias of sources. Television reports have recently indicated that they are showing no bias (being objective) by virtue of presenting two extreme opinions. Objectivity is not determined by matching two extreme opinions. As an example let us look at several different sources. Assume that the topic is whether we should have legalized abortion. The following are potential sources for the speech: a brochure published by Planned Parenthood; the Holy Bible; a publication of the American Medical Association; a book written by a historian at Oxford University (England) about illegal abortions in the United States in the 1950s; an article in *Playboy*, written by Hugh Heffner; and a national poll in *USA Today* that was taken just a week before the speech.

The objectivity is derived from where the information was published, who wrote and/or published it, the background and potential bias of those who wrote and/or published it, and the recency of the material. A brochure published by Planned Parenthood is likely to be biased in favor of prochoice. As one reads through the materials, the speaker–reader should look to see how often the brochure mentions the mental or moral health of the woman who had an abortion. An article published by the American Medical Association may sound objective. What if it is an article about the psychological effects of women who had abortions ten years later? That topic may be good; it may be helpful. Who wrote it? Was it a physician? A psychiatrist? What is the background of the person? How many potential mothers were interviewed? Generally we think that a book published by a historian will be objective, at least more so than one published by individuals in some other professions. However, what if the historian is of a religion that opposes abortion and the book is published by that denomination? Again, how many different situations are discussed? We might assume that an article written by Hefner would be as biased as Planned Parenthood's, but is it? We must read the entire article. Perhaps Hefner has changed his mind since his days as editor. For the poll in *USA Today*, who did the survey? How many people were surveyed? Is the Holy Bible too out of date to answer such questions? These are serious but necessary problems for the speaker to encounter. Perhaps using all of these sources would make the speech more objective; maybe it would not. However, what the speaker does not want to do is use all sources that are biased in the same direction, while stating the potential bias of each. When the speaker finds information counter to his or her own position, he or she should mention it and point out its strengths and weaknesses.

SUMMARY

An effective speech is one that makes the audience members believe in your intent to say something that is beneficial to them. Your credibility is based on your character (trustworthiness), your intelligence, and your goodwill. Goodwill is at the center of the three elements of being legal, ethical, and in good taste. As a speaker you know that you would not like to be hoodwinked by someone who has sold you stolen goods, lied to you, and stated something negative about your family. The effective speaker, then, thinks in advance about what he or she is saying and considers his or her own credibility but also the potential effects on the audience.

APPENDIX B

Evaluation Forms

Appendix B contains evaluation forms for the four types of speeches covered in Chapter 14: the introductory speech, the informative speech or briefing, the persuasive speech, and the demonstration speech. We recommend that the teacher use evaluation forms similar to those provided. The number of points for each section may be adapted for the particular class. The students should be notified about the nature of the evaluation form prior to the beginning of that sequence of speeches.

EVALUATION FORM

THE INTRODUCTORY SPEECH

Speaker: _____

Name of Person Being Introduced: _____

Clearly stated the person's name at least three times:

POSSIBLE POINTS (20): _____

Provided adequate background on person introduced:

POSSIBLE POINTS (20): _____

Provided interesting information about the speaker:

POSSIBLE POINTS (15): _____

Provided clear transitions from one statement to another:

POSSIBLE POINTS (10): _____

Nonverbal communication: utilized effective eye contact. Developed rapport with the audience and the speaker. Illustrated enthusiasm.

POSSIBLE POINTS (20): _____

OVERALL EFFECTIVENESS: POSSIBLE POINTS (15): _____

COMMENTS:

EVALUATION FORM

THE INFORMATIVE SPEECH OR BRIEFING

Speaker: _____

Topic: _____

TOPIC: Is the topic appropriate? Do the audience members already know what is being said? Is the topic too specific for the time limits?

POSSIBLE POINTS (10): _____

INTRODUCTION: Did the speaker gain the audience's attention? Was there a need-to-know statement about why the listeners need the information? Does it have practical applications?

POSSIBLE POINTS (10): _____

BODY: ORGANIZATION: Are there two to five main points in the speech? Does each main point have subpoints? Is the method of organization appropriate? Does each section flow well to the next?

POSSIBLE POINTS (10): _____

BODY: LANGUAGE: Is the vocabulary appropriate for the speech? Are new terms defined? Are there too many new words in the speech for the time limit? Is the speech clear? Is verbal immediacy a component of the speech?

POSSIBLE POINTS (10): _____

BODY: RESEARCH (CONTENT): Does the speech sound like it is well researched? Are sources stated? If so, how many? _____ Is there substantial new information? Are sources up-to-date?

POSSIBLE POINTS (20): _____

CONCLUSION: Did the speech become too persuasive? Did the conclusion bring together all of the components of the body?

POSSIBLE POINTS (10): _____

NONVERBAL COMMUNICATION: Is the speaker using immediacy? Is there eye contact with members of the audience? Does the speaker move away from the lectern? Does the speaker indicate enthusiasm for the topic?

POSSIBLE POINTS (15): _____

OVERALL EFFECTIVENESS: POSSIBLE POINTS (15): _____

TOTAL (100): _____

COMMENTS:

EVALUATION FORM

THE PERSUASIVE SPEECH

Speaker: _____

Topic: _____

TOPIC: Is this persuasive? What is the goal of the speaker?

POSSIBLE POINTS (10): _____

INTRODUCTION: Does the speaker get the audience's attention early? Does the audience understand the need to know?

POSSIBLE POINTS (10): _____

BODY: EVIDENCE/ARGUMENT: Number of sources _____ Are the arguments rational? Is the evidence relatively unbiased? Are counterarguments used to those points against the speaker? Do the listeners appear to be in agreement?

POSSIBLE POINTS (20): _____

BODY: ORGANIZATION: Is the speech appropriately organized to account for those in agreement, opposed, and noncommitted? Does the speech move effectively from one major point to another?

POSSIBLE POINTS (10): _____

BODY: USE OF RESEARCH MATERIALS: Is there a balance in terms of using facts, statistics, testimony, examples, narratives, and so on? Is the evidence utilized effectively?

POSSIBLE POINTS (15): _____

CONCLUSION: Does the conclusion make clear what the speaker wants the audience to do? Is an implementation plan stated?

POSSIBLE POINTS (15): _____

NONVERBAL COMMUNICATION: Does the speaker utilize eye contact and other elements of immediacy?

POSSIBLE POINTS (10): _____

OVERALL EFFECTIVENESS: POSSIBLE POINTS (10): _____

TOTAL (100): _____

COMMENTS:

EVALUATION FORM

THE DEMONSTRATION SPEECH

Speaker _____

Topic: _____

INTRODUCTION: Does the speaker effectively explain why the audience needs to know how to do what the speech is advocating? Has the speaker effectively gained the audience's attention? Is an outline of the speech provided in the introduction?

POSSIBLE POINTS (15): _____

BODY: ORGANIZATION: Are the steps in appropriate order? Are there steps omitted? Are there the appropriate number of steps for the audience to understand?

POSSIBLE POINTS (15): _____

BODY: CONTENT: Is there information provided from personal experience? From outside sources? Are sources stated? How many?_____ Is the information valuable to the listener? Will the listener be able to perform the task? Are audiovisual aids used appropriately?

POSSIBLE POINTS (20):

CONCLUSION: Are the steps repeated? Does the speaker reiterate the need to know? Is the speech wrapped up well?

POSSIBLE POINTS (15): _____

NONVERBAL COMMUNICATION: Does the speaker utilize the principle of immediacy? Is there affinity seeking? Is the speaker dynamic? Does the speaker appear to feel comfortable with the speech? With the topic?

POSSIBLE POINTS (20): _____

OVERALL EFFECTIVENESS: POSSIBLE POINTS (15): _____

                                          TOTAL (100): _____

COMMENTS:

REFERENCES

Assagioli, R. (1973). *The act of will*. New York: Viking.

Assagioli, R. (1976). *Psychosynthesis: A manual of principles and techniques*. New York: Penguin.

Ayres, J., & Hopf, T. S. (1989). Visualization: Is it more than extra-attention? *Communication Education, 38*, 1–5.

Bell, R. A., & Daly, J. A. (1984). The affinity-seeking function of communication. *Communication Monographs, 51*, 91–115.

Buhr, T. A., Clifton, T. I., & Pryor, B. (1994). Effects of speaker immediacy on receivers' information processing. *Psychological Reports, 79*, 779–783.

Christophel, D. M. (1990). The relationships among teacher immediacy behaviors, student motivation, and learning. *Communication Education, 39*, 323–340.

DeFleur, M. L., Kearney, P., & Plax, T. G. (1993). *Mastering communication in contemporary America*. Mountain View, CA: Mayfield.

DeVito, J. A. (1997). *The elements of public speaking* (6th ed.). New York: Longman.

Donohew, L., & Palmgreen, P. (1971). A reappraisal of dissonance and the selective exposure hypotheses. *Journalism Quarterly, 48*, 412–420.

Ellis, A. (1962). *Reason and emotion in psychotherapy*. New York: Stuart.

Fremouw, W. J., & Scott, M. D. (1979). Cognitive restructuring: An alternative method for the treatment of communication apprehension. *Communication Education, 28*, 129–133.

Gardiner, J. C. (1972). The effects of expected and perceived receiver response on source attitudes. *Journal of Communication, 22*, 289–299.

Goss, B., Thompson, M., & Olds, S. (1978). Behavioral support for systematic desensitization for communication apprehension. *Human Communication Research, 4*, 158–163.

Gronbeck, B. E., McKerrow, R. E., Ehninger, D., & Monroe, A. (1994). *Principles and types of speech communication* (12th ed.). Glenview, IL: Scott, Foresman.

Hickson, M., & Stacks, D. W. (1993). *NVC: Nonverbal communication studies and applications* (3d ed.). Dubuque, IA: Brown and Benchmark.

Hopf, T., & Ayres, J. (1992). Coping with public speaking anxiety: An examination of various combinations of systematic desensitization, skills training, and visualization. *Journal of Applied Communication Research, 20*, 184–198.

Hovland, C. I., Janis, I. L., & Kelley, H. H. (1953). *Communication and persuasion: Psychological studies of opinion change*. New Haven, CT: Yale University Press.

Hylton, C. (1971). Intra-audience effects: Observable audience response. *Journal of Communication, 21*, 253–265.

Jacobson, E. (1938). *Progressive relaxation*. Chicago: University of Chicago Press.

Katz, E. (1968). On reopening the question of selectivity in exposure to mass communications. In Robert P. Abelson, E. Aronson, William J. McGuire, Thomas M. Newcomb, Martin J. Rosenberg, & Paul H. Tannenbaum (Eds.), *Theories of cognitive consistency: A sourcebook*. Chicago: Rand McNally.

McCroskey, J. C. (1997). *An introduction to rhetorical communication* (7th ed.) Boston: Allyn and Bacon.

McCroskey, J. C. (2001). *An introduction to rhetorical communication* (8th ed.) Boston: Allyn and Bacon.

McCroskey, J. C., & McCain, T. A. (1974). The measurement of interpersonal attraction. *Speech Monographs, 41*, 261–266.

McCroskey, J. C., Ralph, D. C., & Barrick, J. E. (1970). The effect of systematic desensitization on speech anxiety. *Speech Teacher, 19*, 32–36.

McCroskey, J. C., & Richmond, V. P. (1996). *Fundamentals of human communication: An interpersonal perspective*. Prospect Heights, IL: Waveland Press.

McCroskey, J. C., Richmond, V. P., & Daly, J. A. (1975). The development of a measure of perceived homophily in interpersonal communication. *Human Communication Research, 1*, 323–332.

McCroskey, J. C., & Teven, J. J. (1999). Goodwill. *Communication Monographs, 66*, 90–103.

Mehrabian, A. (1966). Immediacy: An indicator of attitudes in linguistic communication. *Journal of Personality, 34*, 26–34.

Mehrabian, A. (1967a). Orientation behaviors and nonverbal attitude communication. *Journal of Communication, 17,* 324–332.

Mehrabian, A. (1967b). Attitudes inferred from non-immediacy of verbal communication. *Journal of Verbal Learning and Verbal Behavior, 6,* 294–295.

Mehrabian, A. (1971). *Silent messages.* Belmont, CA: Wadsworth.

Mehrabian, A. (1981). *Silent messages: Implicit communication of emotions and attitudes* (2d. ed.). Belmont, CA: Wadsworth.

Mehrabian, A., & Ferris, S. R. (1967). Inference of attitudes from nonverbal communication in two channels. *Journal of Consulting Psychology, 31,* 248–252.

Meichenbaum, D. (1977). *Cognitive behavior modification.* New York: Plenum.

Miller, M. D., & Levine, T. R. (1996). Persuasion. In Michael D. Salwen & Don W. Stacks (Eds.), *An integrated approach to communication theory and research* (pp. 261–276). Mahwah, NJ: Lawrence Erlbaum.

Monroe, A. (1962). *Principles and types of speech.* New York: Scott, Foresman.

Mottet, T., & Richmond, V. P. (1998). An inductive analysis of verbal immediacy: Alternative conceptualization of relational verbal approach/avoidance strategies. *Communication Quarterly, 46* 25–40.

Mottet, T., & Richmond, V. P. (1998). Newer is not necessarily better: Re-examining affective learning measure. *Communication Research Reports, 15*(4), 370–378.

Nathan, E. D. (1964, January). The listening spirit and the conference leader. *Training and Development Journal, 18,* 24.

Richardson, D. R. (1967). Unpublished lecture on Plato, Auburn University, Auburn, AL.

Richmond, V. P. (1990). Communication in the classroom: Power and motivation. *Communication Education, 39,* 181–195.

Richmond, V. P. (1998). *Nonverbal communication in the classroom* (2d ed.). Needham, MA: Tapestry Press.

Richmond, V. P., Gorham, J. S., & McCroskey, J. C. (1986). The relationship between selected immediacy behaviors and cognitive learning. In M. L. McLaughlin (Ed.), *Communication Yearbook 10* (pp. 574–590). Beverly Hills, CA: Sage.

Richmond, V. P., & McCroskey, J. C. (1995). *Nonverbal behavior in interpersonal relations* (3d ed.). Boston: Allyn and Bacon.

Richmond, V. P., & McCroskey, J. C. (1998). *Communication: Apprehension, avoidance, and effectiveness.* Boston: Allyn and Bacon.

Richmond, V. P., & McCroskey, J. C. (2000). *Nonverbal behaviors in relations* (4th ed.). Boston: Allyn and Bacon.

Richmond, V. P., & McCroskey, J. C. (2001). *Organizational communication: Making work, work* (2nd ed.). Boston: Allyn and Bacon.

Richmond, V. P., Wrench, J., & Gorham, J. S. (2001). *Affect and communication in the classroom.* Needham, MA: Tapestry Press.

Signorielli, N., & Morgan, M. (1996). Cultivation analysis: Research and practice. In Michael B. Salwen & Don W. Stacks (Eds.), *An integrated approach to communication theory and research* (pp. 111–126). Mahwah, NJ: Lawrence Erlbaum.

Stacks, D. W., & Hocking, J. (1999). *Communication research* (2d ed.). New York: Longman.

Tannen, D. (1994). *Gender and discourse.* New York: Oxford University Press.

Tannen, D. (1998). *The argument culture: Moving from debate to dialogue.* New York: Random House.

Thomas, C., Richmond, V. P., & McCroskey, J. C. (1990). Reliability and separation of factors on the assertiveness-responsiveness measure. *Psychological Reports, 67,* 449–450.

Treisman, A. M. (1969). Strategies and models of selective attention. *Psychological Review, 75,* 282–299.

U.S. Census Bureau. (1994). *Statistical Abstract of the United States.* Washington DC: U.S. Government Printing Office.

Wheeless, L. R. (1974). The effects of attitude, credibility, and homophily on selective exposure to information. *Speech Monographs, 41,* 329–338.

Wolpe, J. (1958). *Psychotherapy in reciprocal inhibition.* Stanford, CA: Stanford University Press.

INDEX